Flowers in the Darkness

by

Denica McCall

ISBN: 0692441751
ISBN-13: 978-0692441756

Dedication

To my Creator, who has captured my heart and called me to dream with him. Words don't suffice to express all that you mean to me.

To my parents, Charles and Laurie McCall, who I can't thank enough for teaching me the ways of our loving Father and for believing in and supporting the dreams he has given me.

Acknowledgments

I first want to thank my amazing editor, Megan Mulder, for all the time and effort you put into my manuscript. Your professional input and your belief in this project has meant so much. Thank you to my gifted friend, Kendra Cunkle, for your brilliant design! You have made my book look beautiful. And thank you, Jenene Scott, for believing in my project from the moment I shared the idea with you and for all your professional guidance on publishing.

I want to thank those who have read my poems and offered encouragement as well as those who read through the manuscript and gave me wonderful feedback: Mom and Dad, Grandpa Larry and Grandma Mary, Zach and Carly Stratton, Lucie Winborne, and Laura McCoy. Thanks to Brenda McGraw for publishing my poem *Joy* in your book, *Joy Beyond*.

Huge shout out to my beautiful and faithful friends, Denise Sams—who answered my questions about the Genesis Project, and Rebecca Ball—for being such an encouraging writing partner and always believing in me. Your words so often speak straight to my heart. And thank you, Jayne Casper, for all your constant encouragement as well, and for letting me read poems out loud to you. Katy Washburn, I'm so glad we met! Thanks for being an awesome "partner in crime" and for helping me choose the right photo. Lindsay Kathleen, thanks for understanding me and always seeing me for who I really am.

Thank you, Alex Miller, for leading our team on the trip to Pattaya, Thailand, where God did the great work in my heart that eventually led to the creation of this book.

Thank you, Mary Staab, for also believing in my vision and letting me tell you about my crazy idea. You were there from the beginning. And thank you Jackie Morey for your expert advice.

Thank you to all my financial supporters: Claudia, Larry, and Joshua, Kelly Carranza, Ana Augusto, Nate McCall, Dwight and Barbara Cunkle, Marc Smith and everyone who gave at The Hill.

Thank you everyone else who has ever read my poetry or encouraged me in my writing and all those who have believed with me that this dream matters. And thank you readers for your time and investment. I am truly grateful.

Contents

The Genesis Project

A portion of my royalties from the sale of this book will be given to The Genesis Project, an organization located in Seatac, Washington founded by police officer Andy Conner. They have a drop in center open to women caught in sex trafficking who are brought in off the streets of Seattle, where they can stay for up to 72 hours and receive counseling and help finding programs to get out of their current lifestyle.

Their mission:

"The Genesis Project exists to offer hope for a new life to young women leaving commercial sexual exploitation."

Here is a story about how this program has helped one particular woman:

"Abby" struggled for many years with a serious drug addiction which eventually led her into the world of sex trafficking. While she was caught in this life, she was alienated from a lot of her relationships, including her own children. During the whole time "Abby" was being used to sell her body, her mom was praying for her. One day someone in a position of influence who knew of the Genesis Project felt led by God to approach her, and "Abby" ended up at GP. The first time she came, she decided not to stay. But six months later, she called the drop in center and they connected her with a residential program, where she stayed and was able to recover from her drug addiction. "Abby" has not relapsed in over two years. She is now in many leadership roles, employed full time and has experienced some restoration and healing with her family members. God is currently using her to reach out to and touch the lives of many other women who are caught in the life of sex trafficking.

To find out more about The Genesis Project, please visit www.genesisnow.org.

Introduction

I have been captured by a mission.

This mission that has captured my heart has more to do with following the way of a man called Jesus than it has to do with standing for a good cause or leaving a mark on my world. His love has both arrested me and set me free, and more than anything, I want others to know this love.

There is a term that has been thrown around a lot. Something called "social justice." My God is a God of both justice and love, therefore sitting idly by while injustices thrive either under the radar or out in the open is something I just cannot do anymore. I can't let the innocent suffer while I can still do something about it. The people who are harshly mistreated, used, and abused; those who suffer from starvation or sickness because of the part of the world they live in or the family they were born into—they have just as much value as you and I.

When a reality becomes personal, there's no going back to life as it used to be or the status quo. In 2012, I had the amazing opportunity to travel to Pattaya, Thailand, which is one of the worst cities in the world for human sex trafficking and the "sex industry." Many big cities in Thailand as well as the countries surrounding it have made quite a profitable business out of selling sex. I was in Pattaya with a team for about a week. It was enough to shake my perspective and break my heart. Though I didn't go into the darkest regions of exploitation and abuse, I saw firsthand the horrible tragedy that so many women and girls face every day, and Pattaya is only one city. If we think this atrocity is limited to a few unfortunate locations, we are grossly and sadly mistaken.

I like to call my trip a privilege because of the lives I was able to touch, because of the hearts that were opened to me and the healing I began to see in girls who had suffered years of abuse. And because of the new friends I made that I will never and can never forget. These friends are girls my own age who have suffered at the hands of men who only care to satisfy their own lusts. They work in bars in the city as a means to provide for their families living in rural areas far away. Many have children of their own who are being cared for by family members back home. The girls rarely get a day off and very scarcely do they get to see or communicate with their loved ones. I met one girl in particular who captured my heart. Her inward beauty spoke through her outward appearance. I instantly saw a sweet, gentle spirit in this young woman. It struck me that one so used and broken could still offer such a tenderness and sweetness; but you see, that was just who she was. She was a young lady just like me who loved her family and friends and who was holding out for the hope for a better way to make a living yet hardly dared to believe it possible. Because of her situation, all she knew as a means of provision was to allow herself to be bought nearly every night by a man who would not love and care for her, but who would justify his actions on the basis that he paid money for a product.But I did not see products in Pattaya. I saw human beings. Hurting hearts. Desperate eyes. I saw young women who were either terrified or so hardened by pain that some seemed no longer alive. But in each one of them there was yet a spark just waiting to be ignited again by love. Just waiting for someone to tell them what they were worth, that they had value beyond the function and pleasure of their bodies. That they were loved and had something priceless to offer the world.

I marveled at the sacrifice I witnessed in my friend with the tender heart. How willing she was to literally give everything so her family could have what they needed. Members from my team and I paid money to the bar a couple different nights so we could take her out for the evening. We would go buy dinner or ice cream. We were providing the food, so she and her friends could get anything they wanted; it was nothing to us. But she ate sparsely, and she always asked me what I wanted before considering her own order. I was trying to love her, yet she was selflessly offering herself to me.

After meeting these precious girls whom I no more consider prostitutes than any of my friends at home, I cannot be the same. I have to do something for them and for the countless others who are still alone and hopeless, those in my own local community in Seattle who are being trafficked every single day. Though some think they may have chosen this life, no woman truly wants to live this way. It is a trap many feel they have no hope of eluding. So my desire, with the help of the all-consuming love and grace of Jesus, is to bring them hope again. That is my endeavor in creating this book. It is a way to use the gifts God has given me to help those in need. When I start to doubt, I just ask, "Why not?" Why do nothing when there remains the possibility that something good could come of it?

Why not use your talents, time, or means to help someone who is desperately crying out for relief, or for someone who has utterly given up hope of ever being seen for who they really are? These are the questions I have asked myself.

We're alive, aren't we? That means we can do something.

There are flowers in the darkness waiting to be noticed.

Section I. Relationship with God

These poems are my psalms to God. They were born out of time spent seeking him, encounters with him, or moments of just being with him. Some are an attempt to express the intimacy I share with my Creator or the intimacy I long for, some speak of my desire to become more like him, and most are prayers, just like David's prayers and songs in the Bible. I hope and pray these words will resonate with your spirit and draw you closer to our amazing God.

<u>Gaze</u>

Gazing your way in the midst of my day,
This battle inside ceases to rise and have its say
Because when I look toward you
All that seemed important fades away
All my pride and fears are stripped away
So that I can simply be a child of God

In the moment, here with you, loving the one right in front of my view
Not looking behind in regret,
But forgetting my sin as you did
Not peering ahead to see what comes next,
But trusting your plan because you haven't failed yet

FLOWERS IN THE DARKNESS | DENICA MCCALL

When I breathe, your love expands my chest
When I exhale, I let love out again
Peace like a river
Grace like fire
Truth that takes me deeper and reveals that shame was a liar
And I am forgiven
I am free

Simple words and yet so hard to believe
When my mind and feelings rule
Instead of your words that wash through me

Sitting here, I soak in your Gospel
The only thing that made it possible
For my life to have any sense of hope

Jesus, when all is laid bare
I find you're the only thing I care about
So I lay aside my doubt,
The life I want but cannot see,
The shame that taunts me endlessly,
And receive what the Gospel has always been for me
I gaze on you, and I remain free

Anchor

You are my anchor, my steadfast one
Remaining strong when I'm undone
You are the rock I stand upon
When all seems dark, to you I run

Above, above the wind and weather
You and I, always together
When my heart gives way, with you I'll stay
When I close my eyes you hold me tight
Never letting go, even when I lose sight of your view

Oh, Jesus, make me stronga like you
So no matter what comes, I'll hold onto what's true
You are my breath
Your fragrance sweeps me away

13

I am overwhelmed
You're the wind that carries me through the day
To you I pray, it's you I seek
Nothing can keep me from reaching your peak

The strength I have—it's not my own
I am transparent, and my weakness, it shows
But you come and lift me up and shine through my doubt
You make good out of all that is bad; I don't know how
But I know now that you're in relentless pursuit of my heart
And I want you to possess each single part
So my life can stand in the victory you impart

A Child

My heart is bound up
How can I carry yours?
I am not a child but a pauper
Worn out by time and years
Yet you would bring me back
Set me upon your lap
Look into my eyes and say

"You're innocent again
Do you want to run on the paths I've laid out,
That I've set before you to lead you out from your doubt?
I approve of you
You don't have to be shy with me"

I hear his words, stirring in me
And dare to look in his face
I find he's smiling
So I take his hand without shame
And my withered fingers become smooth
With him I can be myself
A child again, with strength renewed
For faith and trust are my weapons in him
And I'm utterly changed when he becomes my strength

So I say
My heart is strong

Not bound with fear, or folly, or doubt
But light with your love

I see with your eyes
And I will tread the paths you have laid out
And seek to grasp what you are about
When I see me through your eyes
I can carry your heart with no shame
And be both a child
And a warrior to bring you fame

Define Me

You are my definition
I had no recognition
Of myself until I saw your eyes
They saw past the false disguise
And all the lies
And set me right

To my disdain
I am a forgetful creature
Who knows needless pain
And then I remember your features
And I know I am defined
By a love that is not blind
For you have seen it all
My selfish, blackened heart,
The fruit in me of the Fall,
But you choose to love just the same
And your eyes transform
Me into what I was created for

To love intently
Bring hope undying to a dying world
Declare justice with my actions,
All with grace and wisdom,
And arms that embrace
Even the most tarnished person
Because what you did I must do
If I am to be like you

15

Your eyes see me this way
An image of Jesus
A matching rhythm to your cadence
A strong, beautiful, firmly rooted
Woman of noble birth
Called to change this Earth

Find

Along the simple, narrow path
I want to find my feet
In your sweet melodic dance
I want to find my beat
You are humble, you are meek
Your voice gently speaks to me

In the whispers of your heart
I want to find my ears
In the love that drives your art
I want to find my years
You are true and you are clear
No confusion and no fear

With the courage in your eyes
I want to find my voice
Against the evil you despise
I want to take my place
You are generous in grace
Keep my gaze locked on your face

With what's good and only right
I want to stand for life
When it's lonely in the night,
I want to find your life
You are strong and you are safe
And nothing spent on you will go to waste

You Saved Me

You saved me
And I just can't rid my heart
Of this flame inside me

That just wants to be a part
Of your great mystery

Your beauty inspires me
To create like you
Earth, space, and trees
Movement, grace, and family
All intricate designs produced
From your melody of life

I want to take what you've given
And express unto Heaven
The joy of my forgiveness
I want to love with an open heart,
Always giving and creating
Never taking or concealing,
Just as you do

You are the beat of my heart
And when I misstep,
I disconnect with the motion that you set

Don't let me stray, I pray
For every day when I live in your way,
I give away your love

Life abundant is what you give
I want it all; I want to live

If my devotion is not to you,
Wake me up
Because my days are few
And I want them to glorify you

Move
Soften my heart of stone
So it beats for you alone
Open my unseeing eyes
So you can guide me on the path that's right
So I can see your beauty is greater

Than anything that puts up a fight

Beyond the realm of fantasy
Your glory,
Your beauty and impossibility
Are what's real

Move me
In your dance
For when I move in your presence,
I know I am alive

You are good news
For we long for something real,
Something beautiful to inspire us
And you are real
Beyond our wildest imaginations
Right here
Right now
Taking us into your heart
To plumb the depths of your love

Open me up
To what is true
Close me off
To what's evil and dark
So I can be the light you speak of

Helpless

Take me off guard
Catch me unsheltered
Encounter me exposed
So I can't resist
But I helplessly melt
Under your devastating pressure
A scream is boiling up
From deep inside
For I can do nothing
Until this intensity subsides
The pain becomes unbearable

18

But I don't want to budge
Until you've done what you came for
And I am utterly undone
Love my dying heart
With your relentless hand
Diffuse the evil within
Until my flesh is dead and you win
Come to me unveiled
So I can see the fierce beauty
Of your holiness and purity
Where all I've done that's good
Is put to shame
Where all I am without you
Is worthless and to blame
I bend involuntarily
While your glory undoes me
Yet I am fully content
For I've been met
By the power of my Maker
By a love this world knows not
And through the pain of my dying
I find life
A life I never knew possible
So meet me unguarded
Attach my heart to yours before I pull back
So I can't breathe on my own
So all I am is all you give
For only in you do I count any gain
Only for you can I endure this pain
Only in your love will I never be the same
You capture me and give me your name

Lost

You fill the sky
With wonderful splendor
The angels sing and stand in awe
Of beauty beyond this world
And I stand speechless,
Lost in your eyes

19

FLOWERS IN THE DARKNESS | DENICA MCCALL

The forgotten sensation
Fills me now
This is what I'm made for
Hold me now
Hold me forever

You fill my heart
With glorious life
I see your world
It lies beyond the naked eye
But tonight I know
You are here
Tonight I know
You have always been near
Times past and times present
And days yet to come
You'll be by my side
Until I am undone

Your mercy undoes me
Your look pierces through me
I cannot retreat
When it is you that I meet,
My flesh protests
But my spirit cries yes!
As you overpower
My soul in this hour

I yearn to know you, God
I want to live with you
Seeing beyond what can be seen
Hearing more than forgotten religion
For you are true
More true even now than in my past

So I will not leave
I will embrace this heavenly beauty
And know the life
That makes me who I am

Longing

My longing heart
Beats inside
Not always steady
But always seeking
For the life that I must find

You are my
Desperation
The fire in your eyes
Fuels my hunger
And I must linger
In your holiness
Until I have you
Until I see
What life is meant to be

You are my passion,
My full desire
I don't want to sit here
And let the lies climb higher
Instead I want to see
The Truth shine brighter

You are my life
And I am finding
That when I know you,
I am my truest self

Let me be lost
'Cause I'm waiting to be found
By a truth and holy fire
That will meet this heart's cry

I don't want to deny
Your power or your love
No limitations will bind
The Spirit of the Living God
And you live in me
This I must really see

21

Help me to believe!

When All is Given
There's a song in my chest
There's a dance in my spirit
An adventurous quest
He's calling me to it

I feel the joy in my heart,
His rhythm in my soul
Now I'll smile and shine
Until I am whole

He has gripped me,
I have been captured
I can spin in his love
For I am enraptured

He's holding me close
But his heart's drumming wild
I can feel his excitement
When I believe I'm his child

His delight pierces
Every lie, every fear
Until I am his
And care has fled from here

His love is breaking through
His truth rules all
When I step off the edge,
He's breaking my fall

My Passion
Beautiful
I want to see you
Your heart beats steady
And I want mine to match
But it wavers
And it fails

Goodness
Holiness
Emanates from who you are
I want to reach,
To touch the pure essence
Of you, God
But I feel I am so far

Can a man be near to God
Most holy, perfect, clean
When he is defiled by shame?
I believe so
But only
Because I know
That The Blood covers
All imperfection
And draws us near

We can be touched
We can flow in the rhythm
Of the heartbeat of the King of kings
Because he calls us his children

I want to touch you
I long to behold you
Draw me near
Oh, Most Holy,
I will worship you
With abandon
Full out expression
Because I cannot hold it in
I love you!

Making Room

In our garden made for two
You asked me to make room
You said, "Open up your heart
It may hurt, but I did the same for you"

And though it didn't seem
There was much room for them
I let the people in
And our garden grew

At times I've asked you why
I must go through the pain
And you remind me again
That you did just the same
You came to love the lost
The sinners, cheats, and liars
And I must do that, too
Or I am chief among them

I've opened up our garden
And I find that when I close the gate,
With even just a little bit of hate,
I can't feel you anymore
But it's never too late
I open up again, feel the pain
And know the sweetness
Of sharing in your gain

Our garden made for two
Is made for so much more
And when I give away
What is really yours
I go deeper in your heart
And love you even more

The Garden
Do you see me?
My heart?
Is it soft as a child's?
Is my hand tender
When you take it in yours?
Or does it resist your pull?
I want freedom,
Liberty,

I want to run in your garden
And catch a glimpse
Of your beauty
I'm looking for you,
Discovering mysteries
Daddy, where are you?
You're here somewhere
I can't wait to run into your arms
And then I'll escape
Laughing
But wanting only
To be caught by you
I'll peek out from behind
Your flowers
Planted just for me
Then I'll dance
In the sunlight
That brightens my eyes
You'll spin me around
I'll have no cares
Just delight
As we roll on the ground together
Lost in wonder
In our love for each other
It's nothing I could deserve
But you make me a child again
A mature child
One ready to rule
But I won't forget to dance with you
In your garden
My daddy
Is the King
And I know I can come
Whenever I please
For I am indeed free

I Need You

I give into you
Do what you want to do

I let go of fear
Won't you take me and draw me near?

I give in
I let go
I don't ever want you to leave
Your words are life
Your words are true
And everything I do
Is nothing
Without you

My heart is yours
That's all you want
It doesn't matter what I thought
Before

You are right
I am wrong
I'm ending this fight tonight
And I'll offer more than a song

Break me down
Hear me cry out
Overtake
Awaken inside of me

Desperation
Is my confession
I don't ever want it to be different
I need you more than anything
Whether I believe it or not

So keep me here
In this place
So I can see you face to face
I would die
If I did not realize
I need you
Father
I need you

All in All

Unimaginable wonder
Unthinkable power
God of love
Coming closer
Responding to seekers

Your strength does not withhold
Your tender touch
Your breath brings life
But destroys the unjust

When we suffer,
You are there
Holding our hands,
Remembering the pain

When we rejoice,
You dance with us
Lead us in your step
For we don't want to fall

Unfathomable Depth
Merciful Presence
Powerful Ruler
We lay down
To give you the place you are due

Heart Fire

My spirit longs to soar
My heart cries for freedom,
Your love to pour through my fingers,
Your touch to ignite souls
You call me to be broken

Broken for the sons
And for the daughters
To be made whole
Love only flows

Through the cracks
That break us open
And expose our pain
My heart cries for liberty
When I see
A brother or a sister
And their destiny

Make me one with you
Make me free to express
The love you put inside,
The fire in my chest
I don't have much
But lack is my greatest gain
For when there's less of me,
More of you is free to be

I may not understand
Your heart's cry
But I know the One who does
So take my hand, and we'll fly!

<u>My Love</u>

I don't want to move
When I'm captured here with you
You show me love is true
And I can be with you
Anytime
Anywhere
My heart reaches out
And you are there
I don't want to move
When you hold me close
Because I can hear your breath

You're more real than life or death
I wish I had another word than love
To tell you what your touch has meant
You go deeper than I ever expect
You know what I need more than I ever will

FLOWERS IN THE DARKNESS | DENICA MCCALL

I want to know your will
Because I love your thoughts
And I don't want to move
Unless I feel your heart
Your rhythm is my guide
When we're one, I can fly

No hindrance, no doubt
Can keep me from these open doors
I am yours
Don't ever let my mouth confess
Anything other than this
I am yours
You make me beautiful
And worth more than I could ever be
Without you

I don't want to move
As I'm here with you
But I will if you tell me to
Because all I want is to live for you
You are my love

Affection

My resistance dies
As I'm met by your eyes
Your embrace inspires
Affection, which lingers in my heart

When I am torn apart,
I melt with every memory
Of the times we've felt
The deepest devotion to each other

In my shifting emotion
I'm found in the motion
Of your dance
Which ignites in my spirit
A fire—can you hear it?
It's raging, exploding

29

With the wildest of pleasures
As I am accepted
By a love beyond measure

I'll be lost here forever
But really I'm found
By a heart so abounding
In love and affection
With pride and attention
I'll stay here forever

My affection,
It lingers, it longs
To be thrust upon you,
The first love that I knew
I always want to be with you

<u>Touch</u>

Touch me
For right now it's what I need

The pain is more
Than this idle sore
You see my need
Your truth I heed
For in this hour
I seek your power

My resistance dies
As I search to find
Meaning in the pain,
Purpose in the fight

I melt beneath
Your gentle hand
Upon the cage
That holds my breath
Upon the home
Where all my thoughts rest

FLOWERS IN THE DARKNESS | DENICA MCCALL

I can't understand
At this point in time
I only hold on
So that light can shine

Everything in me
Wants to run,
Wants escape
I'm a mistake
But I won't defy
Your touch on my hidden heart
I think, now, I can start

Touch me more
It never fades
I want to live loved
The rest of my days

Your Words
Flow through my hands
Like ink through pen
Spirit move me
And do it again

I need your power
To course through my veins
Love spill out on the page
And rearrange
All that I once knew
All that once controlled me
All that once defined me
Because that's not who I am

Spill out,
Tell me the truth

I search,
My fingers anxiously await
What you would have to say,
Not only to me

But to the lonely

Give me the words
To share with the hurt,
The lost, the broken
And those who've been rejected
Show me the truth
So I can pour it into them

My fingers await
Like an eager pen in a writer's hand
For the words to spill out
And replace worlds of doubt,
Of lies, of sickness and drought
May your words bring life throughout

Never Leave
When I am alone
Here with you, I'll sit at your throne
I know that you don't even care
What time of day, as long as I'm here

You draw me in
As if I've never sinned
And all I know
Is I'm your child

There is no fear
Because you want me here
You long to be close
To your creation

Your heart beats
The rhythm of my life
Your message speaks
Of love
You stand outside
Of this space and time
And everything you are and have is mine

What can I say
To the faithful way
You pick me up
When I fall and go astray?
I will never leave you
Never, ever leave you
All I want is to hear you breathe

I will never leave you
For you have never left me
And I know you never will

Open Hand

Jesus, we cry out your name
When there's nothing left, there is you
You hear the cries we raise to you
You see our undying passion
And you beckon us to take your hand
And now we run, hand in hand
As you take us somewhere where you will show us
Secrets little known to man
That you've always longed to share

You're looking for the true sons and daughters
And I don't know what you've found in me
But I know there's a reason you've set me free
And it's beyond me

I'm surrounded by your heart of love
It feels like a suction, like an ocean
It feels like goose bumps, like a drum beating to awaken,
To awaken the life inside we never knew

And we don't know what to do
For we are overtaken
Our very beings have been shaken
By God himself, who became a man
To show us the kind of life we could have
If we'd only hear the unheard sound of Heaven

And take his open hand

Beholding the Face of God
Staggering back as I behold your face
You draw me in with no disgrace
I feel I can't come even though I want to,
Though everything inside screams yes!
I want to be swallowed in your eyes
I'm so dirty, I've lived in so many lies
But you are the Truth, only the Truth
And the Truth is love
Love without recognition, without reason
That will stop at nothing to see that I make it
To see that I live in fulfillment of your words
Whispered in my ears from times past and now
It's a crazy love
But only crazy in the eyes of those who have not seen,
Who have not seen reality as it was always meant to be!
You draw this circle around us
You call us your own
And then you insist
To approach our filthy flesh with your holy kiss
You have us breathe in deep
To choke on your wonder and love
To find new life
That others won't understand
I will come, for I can't deny
This pull in my heart, these tears of joy!
And now I am falling into my Maker's arms
And I finally know who I am

Passion
Surrounded by a force I cannot ignore
It speaks to my heart and fills every pore
I cannot run; it always returns
When my fire goes out, still somewhere it burns
The world would be void without it
A dull place to live, and for my beating heart, unfit
A world without love, without war, without meaning

Nothing to keep my heart beating
Nothing to fight for, to stand for, to be
Without a desire to live, I couldn't be free
But it's here; it will never leave
I cannot escape its grasp
Like a good friend it always comes back
Even when I let go
Even when I don't know
Even when I forget who I am
I turn around and I'm in his hand
And passion flows through my veins again

Raw Love

Aching for this raw love
Unhindered, unchained, undressed
Your real Presence
Enveloped in a shroud of light
Until my heart takes flight
No changing who you are
No disguise
Let me drown in the depth of your eyes
I'm not ashamed—you are my Love
My fear is gone when I'm lost in your song
My own expression weak
How far I've run
Unknown to me, from your true Son
Oh, Jesus Christ, I won't change face
I will not hide your true name
All you've done is love
Your passion haunts my filth away
How can I stay as I was
Lost and only eating dust?
Covering your love
So those who need it most can't see?
Oh God, what do I believe?
I ache for you, and so do they
Unchain my heart, take me away
In your chambers to stay
For in my dwelling near
You'll draw your children here

Our lungs, lifting, deflating as one
Your breath becomes what it always was
My very life, the beauty of being one
Let the rhythm of our beat compel your sons
Who do not know, who cannot see
What their lives are meant to be
Jesus, you're the song, the seed
That goes down deep
And swells and grows into a perfect melody
Calling all the children to burn and be free
I see it now
You're building an army
Of raw lovers of God
Who shine with love and light
And save the nations from their Godless plight
Always bring us back to Love
And may we give it all back to your Son
Oh, my God, you have surely won!

I Am Not Alone

I am not alone
You breathe in me
Jesus, you're my home
You've helped me see
All the brilliant stars
That show your beauty
And the beating hearts
Revealing glory
Hold me close to yours
So I will know
How to love as I'm undone
You have broken me
I want to stay
Broken all my days
So there's a way
For your life to flow
All through my veins,
Out of every pore
And then invade
All the wandering souls

That you have made,
Oh, that you have made
To come back home

I am not alone
You fill my holes
Empty I'm no more
I'm so in love
Oh, God
I want to sing your name,
I have no more shame
You hold my pain
You have saved my tears,
No wasted years
All my life I will
Live to love you more
I am not alone
I'm before your throne
And you've called me friend
So there will be no end
This joy, this hope
Is like nothing I have ever known
Your truth revealed,
Forever sealed
In love

First Dreams

Release what's bound up inside
As my memories crowd out my pride
And remind me you are faithful

Speak to my heart again
The way you did when those first dreams
Were whispers floating through my mind,
Possibilities that could never die

I saw only in part,
In small fragments of time
But now I see
How near you were

The soft whispers of hope
Were not just the dreams
Of an idealistic child
They were the keys
To my present
And what is yet to be

And now, more than ever,
My search is for you
To go deeper and further
To trust like a fool
In the goodness of your heart
And the perfection of your plan

You've woven me in
I can't escape the story
What else can I do
But give you glory?

Release what's inside
Tear down the divide
And make me one
Remind me why I live
And what I believe

To walk on the narrow road
To have passion and be bold
To remember your love and receive
For your love has always been the key

I thank you, God, for truly I am free
May I live this life on my knees

I Wait

I wait
In the stillness of night
With my heart exposed to none but you
And with bated breath
I begin to hear

FLOWERS IN THE DARKNESS | DENICA MCCALL

A faint whisper reach my ear
And I know Love

I wait
With the wintering of my heart,
Alone when no one can hear
And I think no one knows what I fear
Then my veins pump red blood
And I know it's not my own
As I see your eyes
And remember I'm never alone

I wait
Eager, intent on your mouth
For when you speak, I know what I'm about

I wait
Because you are stronger
And can carry me when I am faint
When I have lost all my strength,
My will to fight or go on
And to get through each day,
Then you lift me up

I know you've seen my pursuit
And you know better than I
What I long for in this life

It's you
And when I wait and keep my eyes
Never moving off your face
I live and move and breathe grace
And I can give what I don't have
Because you've touched my heart
Because you are my hands, my feet
And when I move
And smile
And dream
And embrace,
You work in ways I can't fathom

39

And my heart is strong again
When your whispers sink in
And I remember I am saved

<u>Desperation</u>

My heart is bursting, breaking, bleeding
Though silent as a lamb
My soul is seeking, waiting, longing
For the face I once knew so well
My memory fading, but reawakened
As I learn of who you are
Your hands hold firmly, pushing, squeezing
Till my life is no more
I die beneath your touch
Your power nauseates and shocks
But when I open my new found eyes
I'm marinated in pleasure, my soul exposed
My being new, made whole and pure
How can I leave you? How can I run from your merciful hands?
Love without measure became my delight
Why do I resist? Why do I fight?
My forgetfulness reigns, my evil remains
'Till I remember your face, 'till I feel your embrace
My hands are reaching, striving, failing
To do what only your strength can do
So I bow now, utterly lost, totally empty
Of myself, to be filled anew
I'm desperate; I always was
Now my heart knows that it will only grow
If I hold this fact dear and drown in your grace,
I will walk through this life, failing at times
But never ceasing to see your eyes
You've breathed new life into my dying form
We're becoming one as I'm being reborn
And though my sin thinks it can win

It's really a lie for I have said my goodbyes
And now I'm yours, never to leave
Take me, God! Your Truth will set me free!

Love I Can't Resist

I burn when I think of you
When I remember who you really are
Not some image in my head,
Near but really far,
But the Truth that changed my life,
The breath that wakes the dead

My dreams are found in you
I am found, it's true
I once was lost until I knew
The beauty that is you

You steal my breath away
Your glance ignites the flame inside
I didn't know was there
Until you smiled
Because when you smiled, I was gone,
Lost in you forever
I don't want it any other way
You are my Lover, and I'm not ashamed

So cover my disgrace
Make something grow out of this mess
That will show your love, your life, your goodness

I wish I could express
With greater words what all you mean
I long to break beyond the limits
Of my own language

41

And speak to you in heart whispers,
Devoted and sacred thoughts
That only you can fully understand

I am confident
Because you know all things
Even my deepest longings
Which find their home in you

I want to see your mysteries, God
To take joy in the discovery
Of your heart
I'll go where you take me
Hesitation cannot possess me
For I am possessed
By a burning heart
And a Love I can't resist

Never-ending Love Story

Empty me
So I can feel again

Heart is tearing,
Fighting, resisting
Tender touches,
Forgetting crazy love
That imposes,
Threatens to consume,
Invades and takes over
So only one thing remains:
Passion

Longing for love
It's my addiction

FLOWERS IN THE DARKNESS | DENICA MCCALL

But I'm ashamed
Of what every human being craves
But fails to admit

I am the same
And I won't be afraid anymore
To be laid bare
Exposed
To the Creator's hand

He's longing, too
Stronger than I
He'll pick me up
When I feel I'm about to die
He'll carry me through
When I'm empty and dry
He'll be my eyes
He'll ignite me again
When I've come to my end

His love protects,
Lavishes, respects
And won't relent

I am tossed about
By every wave of feeling
And circumstance
But when I feel your heart beating
I fall into step with the Truth
And we laugh together
As we dream about life
We share tears, too
Those times I won't forget
Because they taught me to love

FLOWERS IN THE DARKNESS | DENICA MCCALL

With no regret

So invade my space!
I want to know your face
And fall into your embrace,
Listening to every beat
Of your heart
That beats
Because you're in love with me

I bow
For I am overwhelmed
At who you are,
That you would fall for me
But you have
And your heart leaps
At the very thought
Of hearing me speak
"I love you"

So I'll say it once more
Please hear through my pen
I love you, Creator
More than anything

And you say, "Thank you"
With a tear in your eye
And I won't ever be the same

I melt
At your words
Succumb
To your touch
Your breath

Washes over me
It's like
Nothing in this world I see
And you,
You are here with me
And I'm in love
This is
Our never-ending love story
And it brings you glory

Let Go

This gentle breeze I feel
Comes from my Maker's breath
It stirs inside and awakens
Dreams that once were dead
It's an opening sensation
Like being pulled apart
Painful, but so sweet
For I can't escape the love I meet
The gentle breeze is now a hand
Strong yet tender, with a plan
It's placed upon my heart,
Now squeezing,
It hurts to see I've been so hard
And to feel this pressure breaking me apart
But now I know he won't leave me alone
His love, his sacrifice
Is desperate to release me
So I can love again
So I will feel again
He wants to share his life with me
And he loves me enough to set me free
So stop resisting, stubborn soul
Stop trying to reach unseen goals

Be still, be calm, and believe what you're told
That there was never a love so bold
As to pierce your heart and let desire unfold
Take me now, I'm letting go

Hold Me Now

Like a tender child am I
In the eyes of my Papa
Full of dreams and life
But in him is my delight

I can see it now
His eyes mist over
When he looks at me
And sees my heart

He wants to take it,
Care for it,
Yet gently break it
So it may become
Strong by his touch
But he is my Papa
So I can trust him

I hope we run together
In his fields of grace and laughter
No bounds, endless freedom
Where children of the King
Know their identity

I see that he delights in me
I see it clearly now
He's holding out his hand
Inviting me with a smile

Wanting to take me on a journey
And show me how to love
The twinkle in his eye
Will never go away
If I stay with Papa,
I'll never go astray

Abundant Life

Every movement, every step, every time I take my next breath
It's for you
When I come through that door to new horizons
Expectations rising, anticipation climbing
Worry downsizing my hopes
It's really the next phase
In my journey toward your face
Every challenge, every change
Bringing me closer to why I was made

I learn when I embrace
The sacrifice necessary
To give others a proper place

I grow when I give
When I think outside the box
And realize that this is going to cost

I'm not after comfort
No, I've left that far behind
Though in my mind I find that I'm still blind
Because I still strive to meet that end

But what end is ease?
What consolation is there in peace
When a war rages for this Earth

47

And you've opened my eyes to see?

Everything is for a reason
Every new season
A door, a window into new dimensions
New levels of your presence
And when I don't know why and I can't see how,
I bow
For only then will the mist from my eyes slip down
And unveil to me your plan

What I thought at first, you have torn
Because you remind me that I've been reborn
And every small decision along this path
Will lead me to destruction or to home

If I struggle and fight for contentment in life,
I'll never arrive
Because it's not a destination
But in my determination
And the fire that only comes from your heart
I will press in
I won't give in to the demands of this world
Which push seekers into pleasures that die
Before they ever come alive
No, I'll give up my rights
So that I can have your abundant life

Peace

Sitting here with you
Wanting you but overcome
By abstracted thoughts
Tiny diversions leading to big divisions that cost

FLOWERS IN THE DARKNESS | DENICA MCCALL

I think of you
But from my mind to my heart
And my heart to my lips
This synchronized pattern seems to have a glitch

You are true and pure
And my mind is filled with things that confuse
Things that are useless
Energy abused

But, Father, when I see you and remember
All I want is your nearness,
Nothing can be better
Than resting on your chest

When my world is overwhelmed
With zings of information,
Pull me back together
Calm my aggravation

I come to you tonight
Lost without your sight
As a child needing love
For you give despite the wrong I've done

I am overwhelmed by ignorance and fear,
Refusing to draw near
Forgetting, waning passion
You draw me in, and your peace is my ignition

All In

I'm throwing all in for you
Not caring who sees or who knows
Because when I look in your eyes,

49

I see that my life
Absent of yours will be my demise

I'm running to catch up to you
And as I do you sweep me away
Into your wind, carried by grace
For once I decide I will die to myself
You take my hand and you guide

My joy is complete
In death I find life
And you are my one delight

I'm giving my all for this fight
To see the world through your eyes
Throwing my being into your safe keeping
I trust you, free falling
Not knowing where I'll be landing
Except next to you

I'll follow, whatever the cost
God, give me strength, I don't want to be lost
I don't want to be scared
You've shown me you're there
So take my spirit, body, and soul
I'm giving it all so you can be known

Center of Pursuit

Oh, God, you are my life
So why do I hide in fear and not abide
In the love that overflows from your heart,
Pouring down into empty hearts
Displacing lies and doubts
And showing us what you're about?

FLOWERS IN THE DARKNESS | DENICA MCCALL

I read your words, and then I see
That it's not all about me, and I'm free
Because when I take the heap upon my shoulders,
They droop and sag
Because it's just not meant to be

So today I give you my insecurities
The unknowns, the mysteries, the fear that tries to steal who I am
And once again I take your hand
And run with you in this abundant land
I see flowers bursting up from the once dead ground
Displaying light and life and turning green what once was brown
I see color all around,
Your smile that breaks what binds me to the Earth

So I know what is worth my pursuit
Not me, not them, not what's next,
Not even usefulness
But you,
Who takes everything broken
And makes it all new
Who stared death in the face
And came back to prove
That redemption is possible

So I take your hand
I look at your face
I run this race
With you all the way
Accepting your blood
That eclipses what's maimed,
I get a new heart
That's soft and well trained

I believe and I stand
On your Word that remains
Unchanged

Grateful

I just want to say
In the midst of all this pain,
Jesus, you are still the way
And I'm grateful
I just have to worship
My body has to dance
When I think of what you've done
How you've given us a chance
Free, undone, mercy overtaking
Washing what I've done wrong
Covering me as we're becoming one
Creator, Father, Friend, Provider
You are higher than my words
My creativity lacks flare and power
But when you overshadow
It speaks louder
I'm grateful
I'm grateful that you care
For the little ones down here
That you come and commission
To carry your very nature
And reveal your glory
In color, in light, in words and poetry
Movement, grace, wonder, hospitality
The privilege of this gift
I can't describe
Jesus, I'm grateful for this life

I Close my Eyes

I close my eyes because I can't seem to surmise
What your face looks like when you're looking at my life
I want to see you there in all your glory, just who you are
Pervading every molecule, every moment of this world's time
I find myself catching up to the grind and the design
Of daily life, and I look to try to find
Meaning in the moments,
A reason to create
A song of passion to sing before it's too late
How much time can I waste
Before I taste what I was made for?
Because I'm standing before this open door
Just waiting, listening, pleading
For you to show me how to step through
If I enter will I see?
If I go, will I believe
That miracles direct my destiny?
And you are in, around, and pulsing through me
In this cavity that seems to hold only my organs, blood, and
bones
But in reality is a cave around your Holy Ghost?
What does your breath in me
Feel like? Taste like?
And what should it produce?
When my mind overcomes my pursuit of you
I am lost, and in the darkness I forget
That once your passion flowed through me like blood
Ignited my fingers to release the words that were vaulting from
your heart
Gave me dreams to dance,
To show the world who you really are
But do I know?
Doubt—it leaks in as a tar to my faith

Suffocating the joy that once accompanied grace
And fear displaces joy
But it can never undo your face
Oh, because when I remember,
When I look, when I gaze
And go back to that place,
You're still there
As I sit in my shame,
Feed on my enemy's blame,
You're still there
Holding my hand, seeing my tear-streaked face
And holding my ear to your heart
Just to tell me it beats
Did I forget I'm alive?
This passion you confide, this love that ignites
It's still here
And it's a fight that sometimes is black
That sometimes only shows me my lack
But then grace comes
Like a gentle wave
Caressing my heart and reminding me why I'm saved
And your name is all I care about
I close my eyes so I can see
The beauty that once set me free
Because you said you would stay here with me
Until the night is done, until I see
Until I believe
And longer, you linger, merely to be with me

My Guide
You tell me life can be
So full of joy
I'm like a tree
Planted by your stream

Strong and well fed
My heart, once dead,
Now beats again
And proclaims your hope for those
With eyes to see
I hear your voice and see your eyes
They speak of love, abundant life
So why does dullness creep in, seep in
And seem to steal the life within?
Why am I still blind at times
When your river runs clearly right by my side?
Why can I not see your beauty
When it's displayed right before me?
My fragile mind,
It breaks with big agendas
It falls apart when plans are plenty
And fails to grasp that you are here
To steal the voice from my fear
And give me your hand
So I can follow you and trust again
You speak of love so bold
And demonstrate it every day
So that I may follow you in every way
My fingers find your hand
They're grasping now, so don't let go
I'm trusting you
I'll see, I'll go
I'll follow where you lead
I'm blind in faith but free in life
Please guide me through this day, my Guide

River

My desire grows deep like a well planted seed
Spreading its roots and now flowering

Into blossoms that yearn to go further
To grow closer to you
To dive deeper, love stronger

You come to me gently
You're strong and you're meek
You come where I am
Place your hand on my cheek
You say to me, "Be still,
I'm here and I'm for you
I am your strength
Let my water come near you,
Penetrate the surface
Reach the deep places
And heal as it flows
Let it come
Let it come"

Your sweet peace washes through me
It's your river of life
Reviving my heart

Go deep
Come near
You're all I want to hear
Move me
Kiss me
May your blood flow through me
For I am made new
And known through and through

Steady and Sure

Every time I fall behind or bend under life's weight,
Please remind me you are here

I don't want to deny your attendance in my days,
Your existence in my heart
Please remind me you are here
Not only to stay but here to be my world today
That everything I do would travel a road back to you
That every endeavor, every act, every word
Would find its origin in you
That when I walk and when I talk,
I would think of you and the love that you've shared
Not so I can hoard it
But so I can build a place of safety,
A place of hospitality
Where my whole life is an open book
Ready to draw others into the story unfolding
As I lay down my life for your glory

Let me not look to myself anymore
What I can do, whatever waits beyond that door
The things too harsh to face,
What I try to do without grace
My eyes you train to see you
To be fixed on your eyes that show me what to do, how, and
when
And I will not fade or fall or waste away
When my heart is alive in your constant embrace,
Steady and sure
I'll lock my eyes on yours
So I'll always remember why I was made

Take Flight
"Rest from your striving soul
Give it to me, I'm in control
Of every care, every worry
Everything uncertain in your mind

FLOWERS IN THE DARKNESS | DENICA MCCALL

I hold in a bottle of time
For I stand outside

So
Let go, don't you know
That I want you free?
That my yoke is easy
If you let me carry all the loads, the confusion that overflows
Into your heart,
The sacred place where our love started?
Child, you invited me in
But I can't live in a place so cluttered
With thoughts that are scattered
And not meant to be
Look at me, for I am here
And my very presence in your life
Trumps any fear
That tries to tell you you're not good enough

You're not,
So embrace it fast so I can be
Your everything
Dear one, you are precious to me
I am not mad or absent,
I am fully me
And you see, to be fully me is to be love

I see
Through eyes that wed the dirty sinner
When he was not yet clean
And I see you now
Pure as can be
A child full of destiny
That belongs to me

So come away and be mine
Detach yourself from what binds
And blinds
And find that my life
Flows through and makes a way
For you to not only get through this day
But be alive to my creative design
Take joy and take delight
For even in the fight
You'll soon take flight"

The Middle of this Place

The beauty in the air
Surrounds me until I know you're there
And your love speaks through the wind,
Inviting me to go on this sometimes treacherous adventure,
Where I find your life in the midst of pain
And your breath that inspires me to move,
To push through the darkness in my heart
And as I cling to you, let you wash me white
In this broken place, you receive me
Your heart surrounds mine, and I'm your child
Captured by a love so wild
I wish I had better words
I am astounded that you take my shame
And make me new whenever I call on your name
I'd rather live with you than with me
So remind me to see every time I shift a degree
That you are worth every part of me
Make me a pure vessel
Innocent again, unstained but with your blood
Move my body and my hands
To bring you glory in a beautiful dance
Of life and story

Author of love and life and grace
Just help me to see your face in the middle of this place

Touching

As you place your hand over my heart,
Your river of love washes through me
And life beats again, removing all trace of sin
Peace floods me until I can breathe
In your sweet melody
Gently in and out, my eyes close and I melt
Under the pressure of your hand
Warm and careful, touching what's broken
Healing, watering, restoring
I linger and wait
To know you more
The God who ignites with touch
That makes war with peace
And loves us to our undoing
I lose myself when I'm with you
I can dance all day when your eyes smile
When I know your favor and your laughter
Nothing is sweeter
Than my Creator
May our hearts be close and flow like water
Embrace me, lift me in your dance
So my confession can match your cadence

Truth Meets Desire

The one who sees me sits in this room tonight
The one who knows and looks right through my pride
He is my shelter, glowing heart
A voice that speaks my name
An eye that pierces through my shame

FLOWERS IN THE DARKNESS | DENICA MCCALL

I am here, I am now
I don't know why or how
Creator's breath, Creator's touch
Moves through the invisible
Notes the imperceptible

When I sit alone, afraid of my thoughts
Not wanting to utter the whispers that shudder
All through my mind, the unseen, the blind lies,
He is the one who is privy to my pain
The one who gives me a safe place, who calls me sane

My safety, my guide
Who understands my thoughts better than I
Who calls to my heart when I'm tied by my mind
Arouses desires that stir and make known
The path I long to tread, to love and to yearn

When I don't know how to learn
He opens me up so I can kneel and unwind
Lay before him my pride
The dirt and the grime
So audacious to assume
That my tears could undo
The filth on his feet
But his blood says they do

The one who hears my doubts
When they remain in my head in the crowd
Picks me out, confronts straight up what I'm about
And his words bring me back to desire
The longings that once were on fire
Before they were consumed by my qualms

The one who looks and sees
Pierces through every encroaching disease
And speaks truth that meets
A desire that knows my deepest needs

Life Worship

My hands, they work in endless endeavors
Crafting temporary comfort
Routine tasks that serve to distract my heart from its vulnerability
Probing, finding new enterprises that sometimes mean nothing
Until you rewind me, unbind me, and I see clearly
This invisibility of your faithful generosity
That pumps longing through my very arteries
A blood that is an open sacrifice and from the Cross has spoken
So relativity becomes an impossibility
As I relate to your sensitivity and passion
Overcome and undone, unwind me until you and I
Are one
Compassion compels me, and my knees hit the floor
I can't take any more of this love
And still I fight this war, thinking all my deeds are dead,
That my mind is well fed and yet lacking true bread
Day to day you reveal the futility of my way
And my lack of ability to live substantially apart from your
majesty
See, I know you're the King of kings, Almighty God
And my heart beats in your stream,
Comes alive in the waves that pound over me and infiltrate my
thoughts,
But still I go deeper
With the knowledge that you're the keeper of my accuracy
And all my dreams and desires and every fire that flickers off and
on
Are held up to the light of your Word,

FLOWERS IN THE DARKNESS | DENICA MCCALL

Tested and tried
Until all my flesh is denied,
And I find that my mind can't grasp or reason this time,
When the pressure of your love melts my resolve,
Breaks through this wall I thought was fortified
But was really a paper-thin lie
Your hands, they push and investigate
Every wound, every bruise, every soft place
Every unachieved aspiration
Your healing washes, compresses, brings my muscles, veins, and
bones
Into proper alliance with your Truth
And your ruthless love comes to me again, wraps around my sin,
Choking out its hold
And now I can behold beauty, favor, wonder,
A pleasure of invitation to participate in this astounding banquet,
And you show me every enemy, the miniscule brevity of their
existence
So that all my resistance gives way and I can lean on you in the
midst of the fray
So today, this day, you make me new
Again and again your healing touch
Refurbishes my soul, speaks truth to my heart
That I could only obtain from your impartation
So when I entertain thoughts that market my own gain
Or enlarge my pain, or put down who I was made to be,
Show me your creation,
Your creative harmony you've structured in the depths of me
Parallel to your symphony of love that makes me free
Time after time, remaking and reminding
That faith comes through the edifice of relationship
Built on strong foundations, not on trivial deliberations
That my feeble hands concoct
To turn me away from the worship they were meant for

May my hands, my heart, my life, my deeds, my words
Reflect your beauty, return to their intention
To make weighty your objective of life worship
May veneration and admiration of you be why I breathe

Ignite

God, in you my heart abides
Your eyes always expose all the lies
Your unrelenting gaze uncovers all my shame
So that when I do have to stare my sin in the face,
Your love instantly offers me grace
And provides the only way to be free

When everything is about me,
The chains creep back up and wrap around my limbs again
When my eyes look away, that's when I'm afraid
And all I can do is grasp at fibers of control
That have no substance, no relation to my soul

But when I look at you and let you come around,
Enveloping me with your strong arms,
Breathing into me with your sweet breath,
I let go and find true rest

God, I wish I had deeper words
I wish I had sufficient means to express
What my heart cries
What my spirit longs for

God, if my life and my eyes could just pierce through a mask
My blood, sweat, and tears would be worth every drop
If I could just give you everything and give up
Trying to make everything perfect and right
I know you can use me, empty and broken as I am

To bring healing and love

Because, God, you're not just up above
But you're right down here,
Jesus among us
Your Spirit a flame in us
So ignite

Live Free

Alignment
Under your words, I find freedom
Like the branches of a tree,
They spread over me until all is right
The sun filters through like candles at night
Hitting my eyes just right so I can see

All I need to see is your beauty
Align my thoughts, my ways, my feelings
With yours

When your Truth becomes the only thing
In front of me,
The only thing that brings any peace,
Any solace, any rest from this world overstuffed
With busy meanderings, meetings, and activities—
Truth is my life
And if other things can fade,
If I can let myself wade in the uncertainties they create
And still be calm,
Truth has become my reality, and I will live

Bring my emotions to your Word
Bring my thoughts to your face
Bring my worries to your cross

Take my weary frame and embrace
So that every muscle filled with tension
Every crease caused by fear or pain
Relaxes in light of the legitimacy
Of your perfect reality

You see clearly in my darkness
You know what I need to feel
May I feel as you see
So I can live free

Route of Your Heart

I feel my eyes begin to burn, now shutting out the world
Because as you turn my face to confront your gaze
The things around me fade away
What once held importance has lost its significance
Because your eyes are so magnificent
And my words are so insufficient to explain this moment
Because love is all I feel
Enveloped, consumed, washed through and through
Burning in my bones and veins
Ignition that blazes when you hold my hands
I have so many plans, but when you're this near, all I hear
Is the route of the beat of your heart
And I know that all I want are your desires
Because they are higher
And you are deeper
Crash into and over me with your waves
And as they threaten to knock me over
Let me laugh at the endeavors of my enemy
To take away this chance to be free
To steal this love that's meant to be
Let pleasure wash over me as I open up and see
That your affection is insistent on covering every part of me

66

FLOWERS IN THE DARKNESS | DENICA MCCALL

Of saturating my very pores
So there is no more room for doubts or scores
Under your waves of love I've found what I'm looking for

Section II. Social Justice and the Voices of our Generation

This collection of poems and writings are expressions of what God has begun to show me concerning the darkness, pain, and injustice rampant in our world today. They are intended to expose the reality of the pain and call us to take action and love the world, just as Jesus demonstrated so beautifully when he lived on the Earth and still does now. Let the following words inspire you to give what you have: hope, faith, prayer, money, love, or whatever God may put in your heart.

Reflections from my Experience in Thailand
Written shortly after anti-trafficking mission trip to Pattaya, Thailand

It's hard to believe that it has been nearly a month since arriving home from Thailand. I find it just as difficult to pull my mind away from everything that took place on this trip, even after some time has passed.

Let me paint a picture for you.

Smog. Traffic. Busy streets. Cramped and uneven sidewalks. Open bars, restaurants, and massage parlors lining the streets. A crowded beach right across from a massive, westernized shopping mall. Street vendors everywhere. European and American tourists walking around, most of whom are older men. At night, everything picks up speed. Neon lights, loud music coming from bars, beautiful girls with blank faces lining up outside the bars holding signs. Streets congested with pedestrian tourists. Sexual menus being casually handed out. Chaos. The street called *Walking Street* is like a fair. The sad reality is, everything is for sale at this fair, this feast for the eyes. Not only everything, but everyone. Pattaya is in a sense an amusement park to satisfy every lust. To buy someone in Pattaya is easy, and generally cheap. Slavery is very real there, as it is in America and all around the globe. But when you go to Pattaya, it is all out in the open and buying someone for the night is an accepted practice.

It strikes me how God can break into a city like that. Everything you see around you is so contrary to everything our God stands for, yet he sends us because he knows his light is way too powerful to be overcome by even that kind of darkness. What our team had the privilege to be a part of was to share love and hope with the girls who work in these bars. Day in and day out they are there—they don't get weekends and holidays like us. They work. They sell their bodies because it is what they feel they have to do to provide for their families back home, their young children, and themselves. So many of these women are truly sacrificial, doing it all for the love of their families. I met so many girls who are just like me. Similar age, families they love, hobbies, likes and dislikes, dreams. I found that when I did not allow myself to look at them through the lens of their circumstances or their past, all I saw was a valuable human being, a new friend. In the midst of such perversity, the devaluing of human dignity, and darkness, God really did show up. His love poured through us and into them, and they received it. We were different to them.

I'd never bought a person before. So, in a way, it was strange to pay money to take the girls we met out of the bar for the night. Yet these girls are so used to it, and that fact is heartbreaking. Anyway, we bought them out, took them to dinner to get to know them better, and throughout the week, we took several girls to see the safe house set up by the ministry we were working with, *Not Abandoned*. Just to watch these girls open up in the context of being in the company of people who actually cared about them and didn't want to use them was incredible. The majority of them had never—in their entire lives—felt the kind of love we were showing them. They didn't know it existed until they met us. For the first time, they heard an apology from a man as one of the men in our team felt led to apologize for how horribly men had treated them. That is something they never, ever thought they would hear from a man. But just like that, God broke in. He literally tore down their walls of impossibility and said, "No, it's possible. Here is your hope."

When I started to see things from their side, that's when I was really blown away. Wow. Look what God can do with my simple willingness to go on this trip, with my weak attempt to love a broken person. It worked! And that's when I realized, God loves these people so much more than I ever could. He had them in mind before I ever even cared about the nation of Thailand. He just one day said, "You. You go. I choose you to go to Pattaya in March 2012." I have seen light penetrating darkness. The contrast is so poignant.

I hope what I have shared will spur you to move toward the dreams God has put in your heart. There really is no limit to what He can do. All we have to do is be humble and willing. I am at this point now where I feel like I have to do more, I have to help fight the terrible injustice of human trafficking. I don't know exactly where God will lead me in this, but I'm committing to follow him one step at a time. Through this experience, he has opened up a whole new realm of possibility for me. Things I never thought I would do are becoming a reality. I encourage you to not let your dreams to be too small. Dream big, and if you can't accomplish that big dream today, don't be discouraged. Remember that God is in control, and even when it seems your life is accomplishing nothing at the moment to change this world we live in, know that both your submission to him and your agreement to walk near to him is accomplishing more than you can see right now. But in time, he will reveal. And in time, we will see more open doors.

"...for God takes the side of victims. Do you think you can mess with the dreams of the poor? You can't, for God makes their dreams come true." From Psalm 14, *The Message*

Gravity
With each beating pulse in this cavity,
I realize I'm gaining more gravity

70

FLOWERS IN THE DARKNESS | DENICA MCCALL

For what once held me high in my search
Is now thrusting my heart back to Earth

God, for each tear that you cry on my chest
The whispers don't give any rest
Your love is so deep, so full of compassion
I cannot retreat—you move me to action

Can't I see more of your heart,
Injustice that tears you apart?
The caverns so endless but true
Just let me see more of you

Take me to the place where your tears are held
For every child living in earthly hell
The pain of your love caresses my soul
It's so hard to bear, but you remain in control

So with each beating pulse in this cavity
Help me give into your gravity
For what is holding my ear to your heart
Is compelling me back down where it starts

City in Waiting

A city lies in waiting
Without knowledge
Then a spark in a distant dream,
In a remote corner of a living space,
Sets a fire roaring
Invisible at first,
Its recipient too afraid to share
These hopeful secrets
So distinct, so separate from daily reality
All she sees are glittery bars lining every street

FLOWERS IN THE DARKNESS | DENICA MCCALL

Men who prowl, women clueless
As to the inner turmoil
Of the ones on display
It's a show, it's a play
Let's dress you up, they say
And we'll all have endless happy days
Because don't you know,
And can't you see,
You live in a paradise on Earth?
And there's no place you'd rather be
It's all a joke, it's all a sham
It's a mask covering a dam
About to break loose
And reveal that these colored lights
Do nothing to hide the darkness inside
But she had a dream,
A ray of light streaming through her broken mind
Tempting, telling of things to come
Or perhaps, wonders only hoped for
Until one day,
It all really did change
A group of people, nondescript
Broke in as if they belonged
They were not dead, they were alive
They seemed to know a real light
And wanted to share with those who would see,
Who were tired of their exhausting reality
She saw them come, she heard the dream
Come back into her memory
Crowding out every lie and every enemy
Of her heart who only wanted to feed
And leave her back at the start
With no life, no love, no hope to move forward
But could this be—

Could they be different?
Could it be more than a dream
Of a helpless woman who could no longer see?
What love was this—
What hope shone forth!
They held her heart
As if it held infinite worth
And broke open the dam of her tears
Which were hidden in shame for all those years
They understood
How could they know?
That one dream she had was her only hope
And now it had come true
Out of this army of love
Willing to come
To share with the one lost soul
In this city in waiting
Who was ready to hear a voice tell her
She was worth saving

Promises

With promises you found my innocence
With dreams you crushed my future
With knowledge of freedom you removed my reticence
And now I'm locked into this broken picture

Just one more face in this city of disgrace
Just one more soul so far away from home
A girl no more, I'm a woman in this place
I've sold my heart though not fully grown

At first I felt it all, like the ripping of my flesh
The pain, the brokenness, the lonely days and nights
The brutal treatment breaking my spirit

FLOWERS IN THE DARKNESS | DENICA MCCALL

'Till they stripped me of my fight

I finally let go so I could survive
Now I don't feel at all because if I do
My tears would fill the night
And steal my chance to earn what I am due

At sixteen my husband left
Abandoned with one son
At twenty now I'm here
Most nights with more than one

I'm wanted once again
They use me up and leave my heart for dead
We try to be strong, my girls and I
Though our shared company can't keep our souls fed

Please find me
I don't know where my innocence has gone
I'm just a kid, you see
I don't know how life has gone so wrong

I'm scared to grasp at hope
All words have proven empty
Who can lead me home?
Who can help me feel my heart beat?

<u>Hope</u>
Can you hear me?
I just want to know
If anyone out there knows
Who I am
I'm not the girl you think
My heart has died
And I can't feel anymore,
Not like I used to

74

FLOWERS IN THE DARKNESS | DENICA MCCALL

My body contracts without tears
I've been here too many years
Would you recognize me
If you saw me now?
I don't know
I barely see the light of day
They tell me to stay and I do
Not because I want to
But because my will perished long ago
The only will I have is the will to live
But even that is fading away
Am I anything anymore?
Does my voice make a sound
As I lay here on the ground?

What's this I hear?
What's this I feel?
A tear, pushing itself through?
It can't be, no!
I won't cry, I won't grasp at absent hope
I used to do that
Until I started to believe what's real
That I will never be saved
I'm a daughter, you say?
Whose?
My father disowned me
Nobody loves me
But I feel your hand
It's gentle,
Compassionate
Is it really for me?
You love me, you say
You love me, is it true?
Don't do this to me
My heart is already torn in two!

I'm rescued, I'm saved!
I never believed in this day,
But you broke the chains
And I am breathing again

Oh, it's been so long
Can I ever be
The little girl I once was?
That and more, you say,
And I trust you
I am free

My Generation

I can feel the desperation
Seeping through my pores at night
I can hear my generation
Hopelessly dying in their plight

I can sense anticipation
Growing stronger in my veins
I know there's a visitation
Coming down to heal the pain

Hearts are breaking
Hands are shaking
People searching
For true life
Desperation
Is our motivation
To deny
These tormenting lies

I can't get you off my mind
For you're the only one who died
To save a people lost and blind
Children of a Father who is kind

I'm crying
I'm pleading
I'm screaming
Oh, come inside!
For my generation
Is hungry
For your life

Silent Cries

These silent cries
Come from deep inside
These desperate screams
Lack a voice
These eyes, they speak
More than words could tell
How will they see
That they can get out of this hell?

The tears, they fall
One by one
For every broken daughter,
Every longing son
For all they ever knew
Was everything that wasn't true

These hands, they reach
For something real
These hearts, they bleed
What do you feel?

These bodies ache,
These lives at stake
What will it take?
Have we made a mistake?

This place is dark,
So void of light
With every heart
Bound in utter fright

Bring forth the day!
Lead us out of this fray!
Stop the pain
Right here, we call on your name
Right now, where we're at, we pray
We want to hear what you have to say

The Cry of Our Generation

Passion fills my every pore
A longing too intense for words
I'm hungry night and day and nothing fills
Not the bottle, the lovers, nor the pills
I know I'm here for more than this

Dreams fulfilled in stories aren't enough
Tales of sacrifice and heroes fill my nation's past
But there's a great divide between now and then
And here I am
Born into a world lacking true men and women
I can't deny the thirst that consumes my dry bones
Someone pick me up and show me home!

Someone tell me I'm not alone
The only one? I don't know
But I can't help thinking others feel it, too
The ones I pass at school,
The employees at my job
My friends who like to party on days off,
Do they see my cry
When they look into my eyes?

I go chase fame, they root me on
But is their cheering merely noise to silence what's wrong?
I see my future—half-veiled, but something's off
It's not long enough, you see
Someday I'll die
And all that's left will be the ones I left behind
And then what?
Do they get the same life I did?
What did it accomplish?
What did I do?

You see, I'm looking for something true
My energy creates, my emotions consume
But what of it
If I'm missing something huge?
My soul tells me there's something I don't know

FLOWERS IN THE DARKNESS | DENICA MCCALL

Someone help me find it, please
So I can stop chasing after the breeze
I want to leave a mark that's more than me

Found

In my mind, I see your face
I remember how you were found by grace
So close we were in that place

Now my heart recalls from far away
The beauty of two broken souls
Brought together by the One who knows us all

When I think of you now, I feel pain
And wonder if you're okay
I should know you are,
For we have a Father who never stops,
Never rests, and never forgets who his children are
Or where they might be

In this foreign country, my heart found a place
And you a piece in mine
I can't get you out of my mind
Because I can feel the love of my Savior
Reminding me he's good and he's kind
Don't be afraid, dear friend

God has you in his hand
I know this is true,
He'll never stop pursuing you
Our memories may fade,
But he makes them bright as day

We can't forget the reason he came
So all may know this love that overcomes shame

That gives hope in the middle of unrelenting pain,
Light that pierces through the darkest of streets,
Peace that lets our heads rest on his chest
And dream of the life we may not have yet

But you are found,
This I can never regret or forget
This I pray you carry in your heart
And know that in him we are never apart

I didn't know you for long,
But he has united our song
Into the harmony of the lost but now free,
Don't ever doubt who you are meant to be

The Edge

I saw you on the edge
Partly out, partly in
Not wanting to pretend
That your desires wouldn't win
I could see beyond
Though you didn't know
My Father helped me see
And gave me courage to come and show
A love worth living for
So you would know
Because he died for you, not just me
I wanted you to believe
I saw it in your eyes
The longing too deep for words
Your smile gave me joy
I knew he picked you out
And you were always his delight
I don't know what they've done to you

FLOWERS IN THE DARKNESS | DENICA MCCALL

You don't have to share
As long as you can see now
That someone always cares
I don't know your past
Or comprehend how our paths met
Except that it was in his plan
And now you understand
That we're sisters always
Both, in the palm of his hand
Through pain and tears
And joys and fears
We're not alone
Together we can stand
So far away, in different places
But our hearts belong to the One who made us
Mine bursts with gratitude
That he would send me to help find you
You are lost no more,
Not a victim of this storm
Whatever life throws your way
Remember that he's there to stay
And he always has a way
To bring you home to him
I saw you that day,
A child of his grace
And that will never change,
For your eternity has been replaced

Give

Give until you break
Give until it hurts
Give until all the little pieces of your heart
Are spread across the world

FLOWERS IN THE DARKNESS | DENICA MCCALL

Give when you don't get
Give when you forget
Give when you don't know how
To give anymore

Give
Break
Love
Forsake the selfish cause
Of yesterday's pain
For someone's heart is at stake

Love like it's your last,
Your last chance to make a mark
On a desperate heart

Love until all the beats
Die away
And you are left
With one mere breath

Love
For this is your holy calling
Will you rise up
And take the leap?
If you need incentive,
I'll tell you a story
Of a King who gave up his glory
To love the lowly
He died, you see
To set you and I free

So give
And love

Even when you can't bear it
For there is someone there to share it

Broken Child

Am I a broken child?
Or is it the little girl on the street
Selling herself over and over
'Till her heart no longer beats?

She smiles only to put on a show
A survival instinct to avoid the blows
Her face hurts for tears holed up inside
She can't release until she's alone in the night

Agony and shame
Follow her every day
Consuming pain is what she feeds upon
Even when all the men are gone
Because she thinks no one cares,
And no one sees her misery,
Her world is shattered and insignificant

Who would see a girl like her
And see something innocent?
She is so lonely, she fears
She won't survive many more years
Why was she born into this world
To be a toy played with and abused?

All the thoughts in her brain are confused
All she's known is being used
Is that what she is good for?
Could there ever be more?
Will her heart always be sore

FLOWERS IN THE DARKNESS | DENICA MCCALL

At the end of the day
After everything has been stripped away,
Though already she was raw and wounded?

Is there good in the world?
There isn't in hers
Isolated, lost, broken child,
We all are to some degree,
But what if what we've been helped to see
We could bring
To this child torn apart?
What if she could know hope again
And feel her beating heart
Awake with life,
And purpose to go forward?
What if your story
Could be the healing balm
To rub away the shame
And tell her it doesn't have to always be this way?

Am I a broken child?
Yes; are not we all?
But so is the one on the street
So let us move our feet

Entombed

Deadness entombed inside of their eyes
Numb to the icons that once prompted fear
Hearts beating, but captured by meaningless lines
My own mind bolts from the garbage these children hear

Little eyes, little ears
Small minds but big dreams
Consumed by a fantasy that demeans

FLOWERS IN THE DARKNESS | DENICA MCCALL

The purpose of life, of love,
Of family

My heart is broken inside of my chest
I can change the channel but I can't change the rest
Dirty thoughts, ruined deeds
Growing up no longer feeds
Maturity
But instead we breed
Independence, lust, and greed

The making fun of family
Overshadows their need
To be heard and to be loved
To belong and blossom in safety

A healing eclipsed by comatose pleasure,
And by what do we measure
The success of a man?
To make money, to have fun?
Tell me, what is our plan?

Children are learning, coping, changing
In this prison of media that replaces community
What must we do for them to be free?
Let's take a stand so they can be who they should be

Reborn

Words on a page generate insufficient aid
When the whole world's a stage
Wrought by lies liquefied to entertain,
People demanding perpetual production
For nothing more than consumption
A venture to fill a gaping chasm inside

FLOWERS IN THE DARKNESS | DENICA MCCALL

That only grows with the passing of time
Sitting down to unwind, ingesting line after line
Image after image
Word after word
Rhythms that classify millions of jaded lives

People are bottomless mines,
Filled up with dreams but lacking clear guides
Searching for pleasure hour after hour
Wanting a name, a worth, to have power
But never satisfied

Media has redefined our institutions
What once was family is now insanity,
What once was love is now human sympathy
Mediocrity, momentary intimacy,
Which has led us down the path of depravity
When laughs are elicited
By making fun and offending
Those who are different,
There is something we're lacking

Why is our culture unhappy?
Fake smiles and gestures brighten the day
Only to go home at night and turn into shame
When money and fame become the new game
True life is melting and slipping away

Their fingers outstretched, grasping at air,
For what they thought was surely there
Hidden inside the glamour and glaze,
Is merely a pocket of nothingness that only serves to darken this
maze

FLOWERS IN THE DARKNESS | DENICA MCCALL

The eyes of the crowd absorb whatever is thrown their way
Even shams crawling straight from the grave
And what has our money attained?
Only more cravings than our fragile hearts can contain

Our words, insufficient
Our visuals, noncommittal
Our movements lack vision
The acts, the plays, empty as our graves
Beauty is fabricated from minds enshrouded and blind

To be renewed, art, like us, must be reborn

Conceived in the heart of a King:
Movement, grace, and beauty
Words that connect, mingle, and create
Songs, poems, and stories that bring dead hearts awake

Art that explodes beyond the four walls of the box
Creation that floods and brings life, breaking locks

Dance that moves beyond physical realms
Healing the broken with each turn, jump, and sound
Music that pumps red blood through our veins
And reminds us with each refrain why we were made

Formed in the heart of a lover
Our insufficiency is covered
As we surrender our inability
He comes and teaches us how to breathe
And creation becomes an infinite symphony
To bring honor to the King of kings

Ignition begins when we pick up not only a cause but a cross

FLOWERS IN THE DARKNESS | DENICA MCCALL

Giving our hands, our minds, our hearts to be holy
The Creator takes each limb, each tear, each part of our shattered
stories
And gives the world what they could never find seeking their own
glory
Releasing, redeeming, redefining
Breaking this cultural normality out of its prison,
Artists create and life has been given

Mark

The cinder of our dreams still waits
In the caverns of our hearts
Where all that's alive is hidden

We feel a spark until fear lifts its head
And tells us no, it's too big
Push it down and get ahead,
Yet we fall behind
Because what makes us come alive
We've told ourselves has died

And so while we move up, move on
Climb ladders, push past those who get in our way
To make sure we're safe,
What the world needs lies dormant in our dreams,
The dreams of a child
When we thought we could make the world a better place

But we were foolish, then, right?
We didn't know wrong from right,
Real from imaginary

But what if every visionary
Gave up their fight

FLOWERS IN THE DARKNESS | DENICA MCCALL

And let the sparks die with their dust in the grave?
What inspiration would we have today
To become better people,
Have compassion that brings change?

There's an ember inside, you know it
Am I the only one
Who is trying to release
These longings inside that don't yet have a voice?

There is something in all of us
A deep seeded dream
A vision of greatness
That must be redeemed

You've been told it's too much
You've been told you're motivation's not enough
They've pushed you down, torn you up
Said that giving up will be your only hope
To make it, to get by

But aren't you sick of getting by?
Aren't you weary of activity with no life?

There's a spark inside that ignites
With certain words, pictures, stories,
Conversations where deep meets deep
And reveals truth where doubt has been your meat,
So let it come alive
Let the whisper inside become a shout
On the hilltop of your creative destiny

Don't think there are too many dreamers out there
And you're not the one to take a stand,

FLOWERS IN THE DARKNESS | DENICA MCCALL

Because that something inside *will* die
If your whole life it is constantly denied

Acknowledge the cinder
And let it grow bigger
For our Creator did not give dreams
To be seen but not revealed,
Admired as children but not inspired as adults,
Felt but not acted upon

A passion without action
Will only lead to the death of your soul
What the world needs are those who will be bold,
Bold enough to speak the crazy thoughts,
To begin that dangerous journey
When they can't see the end

Will you be the ones to forsake the status in which you've been
placed
And take your rightful stake,
Thrust it in the ground that you've always stood upon
But were never satisfied with
To make the mark that's yours to make?

Thirsty
It began as a seed withered in her soul
Once alive, holding thoughts that no one ever knew
A child's hope evaporating
As those around attacked the dream
And now the seed sits, black but still felt
Waiting for a drop of water
To expand it
Push out the props
And hold love that's real

FLOWERS IN THE DARKNESS | DENICA MCCALL

See, her world is not ideal
Like she makes it out to be
Her love is not real
Like she's been made to believe

It began as a dream shattered by his reality
Lofty ideals and intentionalities
Pulling together, building a ladder
Yet dragging him down with the current of status quo
He never wanted this story
He only wanted the glory
And now he's knee deep in a heap of deadlines
And numbers
That do nothing to gratify
The longing inside to belong
And now, just one drink will do
To humidify his wrinkled heart
Cast off weariness and become a part
Of a family

It began as one soul covered in pride
On the outside glad to be alive
Yet, stripped and left alone
With nothing to own and no one to hold
The spark of life inside died with his pride
Begging for mercy, bereft of dignity
The people pass by uncaring
And he wonders if they see a person
Or a life snuffed out by the way he's been living
And he knows that just one penny,
One kind eye,
Will quench the thirst he feels inside

It begins with a family

FLOWERS IN THE DARKNESS | DENICA MCCALL

Of sons and daughters,
All adopted by a father of royal birth,
Who each know love because they never deserved
This kind of mercy
In return for their rejection, pride, and selfish schemes

It begins when one reaches out a hand,
Touches that seed with a word that brings life
To her heart wrapped in death
Pursues without rest to free his crushed chest
To bring hope to his frame again
Notices the man whom the world has forgotten
Beaten and robbed and broken
And offers the one thing he needs to be free,
A drop of water
To satiate the thirsty

Section III. Called Up and Going Forward

These are poems that speak of victory, dreaming, and becoming who we are born to be. Some of them are declarative, some speak of the longing in my own heart to stand up in courage and take risks, and some are written in God's voice as words from his heart to us. I begin with a story that illustrates what it might look like to take the risk to be different from the crowd when compliance is expected but you know you were made for more.

<u>Dance Hope</u>

She stopped in the middle of the crosswalk and became a silent, unmoving stone with eyes. The cars waiting at the red light probably wondered why this young, ordinary looking girl had stopped mid-commute among all the other "fish" of this great pond. But she was compelled to. Something wasn't right. No, that wasn't it. Because a lot of things hadn't been right for a very long time, and day was beginning to break inside her heart. People passed the breathing, seeing stone. People seemingly on a mission. Some appeared to have a one-track mind—striding toward a destination seen in their mind's eye that crowded out every other image. Some looked lost, some looked happy. But it was only momentary—it was always momentary. So many colors flew past her, so many different kinds of people, all with varying gaits. Some were silent, like her, and some couldn't seem to pull themselves away from gabbing nonstop into their ear devices.

She looked up—the sky carried a grayish tint. Smog they called it. The sky was like a canopy, absorbing the chaos of the city because it had nowhere else to go. Horns blared, engines rumbled to life, sirens called from a distance. Dried leaves flew past her, and her long hair was picked up and gently set back down again, as if a hand had done it on purpose. Everything was moving. Everyone was impatient, restless. She could feel it in her bones, but she herself fought against it. No one took the time to stop. No one was courageous enough to face the reality of what was really happening. So many different stories buzzing around in this one busy city, but no one knew who the person beside them was. So many lives all mixed into one, all inevitably brought together by the day and the tasks. But no one knew. And no one cared.

"So many people need hope. They all want to believe someone cares," she muttered to herself, breathing in the almost toxic air. Toxic to those around her who knew nothing else, but life to her, for she was being awakened. She had to do something. Did she have the courage to stand out, to not take the easy way and become part of the unnoticed blended mix?

Dance Hope.

The words rode on the Autumn breeze, which picked up her long brown hair again so that it streamed behind her. A deafening horn blared in her ear. The light had turned. She had a choice to make. She turned to face the cars, full of the impatient people all needing to get somewhere. They were yelling and cursing, but the girl's eyes filled with compassion. They needed hope, and she was the one to give it. After all, it was her name.

Hope stripped off her gray coat, revealing a flowing white blouse and a red scarf that the wind began to toss around. In the middle of the cross walk, looking straight ahead, she thrust both arms out to either side of her, palms facing out.

Hope was driving away the encroaching darkness by that one move. She thrust her hands downward as she jumped out to spread her legs. Then she bent one leg and lifted it, sending her arms both out to the right, looking to the left. The music that led her came from inside but blended with the rhythm of the city. The beat she heard slowly infiltrated the city as she continued to dance.

She swirled around with her fingers spread and her legs

following one another in the air. The wind swept the red scarf in pulsing ripples. Hope continued to dance as her lungs filled with more and more sweet air. She became a moving piece of art, a splash of light in a dull city. People gathered around, all in awe of the beauty before them. They looked on and every heart longed to be free like that, to have that kind of courage to do what they were always meant to do—that tiny whisper echoing from childhood memories, from dreams shot down long ago.

Every movement that Hope danced, she released what her name proclaimed. She was doing what she was made for. Consequently, not one person who watched walked away unchanged. There is something that calls to the deepest places of others when even one is bold enough to take a stand. And that is what happened that day.

Hope listened to her Creator above the rest of the noise and changed the city.

Forever.

Darkness Aside

Darkness aside,
We live in his light

Freedom pursues you
For we won't give up
You may not see us
But we're here
Training in courage
Receiving endurance
Running this race set before us
You think no one cares
But our hearts break
You think no one hears
But you have our ears
We are the new breed
The people of light
And though we're not perfect,
We live for this fight
In your darkness, in your night
He will break through
He will find you

Listen, all you children of the King
He's sending forth a new sound
Hear it ring!
He's opening up hidden places
And leading us to new faces
The ones who are waiting
The ones forgotten
His thoughts are toward them
So be his voice, his love
Reach out your arms
And burst forth out of your gloom
For your darkness is light to them
A hope beyond hope
Don't wait till you're all new
Go now, for only the used can be used
We are qualified by the Cross
So put discouragement aside
Be who you were meant to be
And in his grace abide

Darkness aside,
Awake to life!

Cry for the Sound of Heaven

What are you saying?
What are you doing?
'Cause I've got to know,
I have to know
For this fire inside will not burn out

My seeking heart is getting closer
Closer to answers
Closer to reality
But there is so much more I can't see yet
But please, I want it
I want it more than my next breath

This desperate child is on her knees
On her face seeking you

FLOWERS IN THE DARKNESS | DENICA MCCALL

My heart won't shut down
Not until I've found
The love I was made for
The purpose to die for

My desperate soul is crying out
For touches of Heaven
For touches of freedom
And I don't want to move
No, I don't want to move
Because I'm right here with you
Just beginning to see

You've brought me through so much
And I don't deny what you've done
But my heart has died momentarily
And I need a permanent resurrection

I'm made to live with passion
Who cares if I'm different from this world
I'm meant to jump off this cliff
Deny myself
Let go of these lies
All I want is the Truth

So I'm seeking your power
A desperate child on her knees
On her face
And I don't want to move
I don't want to move
Until I see your face,
Know your love
And am sent on my way

Give me the words
To open up the lost
Give me the touch
To embrace the broken
Give me the eyes
To see what you see

97

Give me the ears
To hear the sound of Heaven!

Impossible Dreamers

Move my heart to flow in your life
Rhythm of my soul,
Blow and make me whole,
Wholly yours
Holy, yours,
I take your blood,
Receive what you've done
So you may be
The breath in me

Speak, Father,
Tell of your plans
Kindle your sons
To awaken the land!
Reach deep,
Enliven dead places
Your glory to conceal
Every darkness in my face

Enlighten
Revive
Stir up
Burn alive
One desire
Forever fire
We are yours
Your impossible dreamers

Children of Light

I want to know you,
It is my deepest need
Can I behold you
So the children can be free?
I want to hold you
But will you be held by me?
I'm not the only soul

Who has felt all alone,
Who's known the pain of rejection
Or the fear of imperfection
It chases me
Every day
It wastes me
'Till I can't go on another day
Do you know,
Do you know how to live this way?
We were the darkness
But now we're the children of light
We're in a battle
Waged in the darkest night
How can we see and not cry?
How can we live and not die?
Oh, when the stakes are so high
How can we sit idly by?
Passion calls us
Pursuing, arousing
Calling the light inside
To be what it first was
Heaven is calling
Heaven is falling
Down to Earth
And we, immortal, do birth
Your hope where there is none
We do what cannot be done
Because you already sent your Son
And we want to know you
And the only way
Is to embrace the ones who lost their way

Speak Through Our Hands

You cry for freedom
For the children in your Kingdom
And on the outskirts of town
They can also hear the sound
It's for them, it's for us
A heart of compassion, of deliverance
And you've chosen our hearts

As a bed to weep upon
A chamber of secrets
A vault of strategies
To reach the outsiders
Who are lost in tragedy
Freedom we hear
Freedom we shout
So those who aren't near
Will know what you're about
You're kind and you're good
You're gentle yet strong
We're wrapped up in your song
You sing, "It won't be long
I'm coming, dear child
Wait and take courage
I won't leave you alone
When it's dark and you're cold
I'll come lead you home"
He speaks through our hands
He loves through our words
So open each finger
And speak what you've heard

Not the End

Taking up the battle cry
Free the slaves, don't pass them by!
We're waging war, joining the fight
Don't let it slip your mind

How can an army rage
Against an enemy so great
When hearts are not as one
And lives are not surrendered?

Is this a cause worth fighting for?
Is it worth your life, your everything?
It is not something to trivialize
When so many lives are on the line

FLOWERS IN THE DARKNESS | DENICA MCCALL

Make us one, great Father of justice
Maker of every heart
Healer, lead us on
To leave it all on this battlefield

Our movements take flight
To break chains of those out of sight
Our given hearts change lives
When our eyes are fixed on what's right

So when it's hard and you don't feel
Like fighting anymore,
Or training all the way,
Remember that you're chosen to prepare a way

Dancers leading forth
Stepping into the fray
Stomping out injustice
Don't let your devotion stray

God has given us the day
He's given us the task
That seems so big we make no dent
But, chosen ones,

It's not the end

Rejoice
We are broken
But he is whole
It's time to rejoice

We are whole

Because he was broken
It's time to rejoice

We live in lack
He is our life
It's time to rejoice

Our weakness is evident
His strength overcomes
It's time to rejoice

Open up your heart
Search the deep reserves
Remember how he loved
When you were once reversed

Think on what he's done
Look upon his face
His eyes are toward you now
His favor still remains

We are faithless
He is faithful
It's time to rejoice

We are dead
He is alive
Awakening us to new life
It's time to rejoice!

Tree of Life

Before my eyes the Tree of Life
Stands unmoving, stark against the twilight
Not far beyond another is rooted

FLOWERS IN THE DARKNESS | DENICA MCCALL

The Tree of Knowledge, how good its fruit looks

I've heard talk of a narrow road
Where beauty has yet to unfold
Where fruit is not visible to the naked eye

And then there is a road where the way is wide
It waits, inviting weary travelers to traverse its path
Its beauty beckons, its members smile
Making it appear the better choice

But have you heard the voice that calls to the deep
And opens eyes to see reality?
For if we follow what we feel
Or what seems real
We'll miss the beauty of his life
We'll pass up the chance to drown in his laughter
Along the way, we'll know true grace
But the wide way only leads to disgrace

For when we find our self falling on our face,
The smiles disappear, the beauty fades
For momentary appeal never stays
The road may have been open with ready arms
But only for the good who wouldn't do any harm,
And we are all prone to fall

The narrow road looks closed and cold
But if we only knew of the love we would behold!
For in fact this road only leads to one tree
The Tree of Life, you see, where we'll know mercy
Not under the law, not striving to be
But becoming more like him, whom we're made to receive
And reflect so that others can see

FLOWERS IN THE DARKNESS | DENICA MCCALL

This tree that holds the infinite beauty
That can never fade, never grow old
And the fruit that goes beyond what the eyes can see
Into the deepest of our deeps, pure reality

The question will always be: what will we choose?
Neither road makes an easy journey
But which is more worthy?
To walk with him—with Love himself, with grace that abounds
Or to walk by ourselves, alone in a crowd
Of well-wishers who don't mean it?

I don't know about you
But I know now what's true
I want to be found, pursued
Not misconstrued
And made to believe a lie
And make up a life
To try and fulfill
What I can never have for real

The narrow road leads to life
A life that's not even mine
But is freely offered
To all, to have what their hearts have always recalled
From times not remembered but felt
The realest of real

So there stand the two trees
Not far apart, but at the end
Of two different roads

Let's choose to be free

<u>Awakening</u>

Awakening
It's starting inside
What's dead is coming alive
Deep down
There is a cry
It's coming up again
Peeling back the layers
Coming back
To what really matters
These thoughts in my head
Try to overtake
I've made too many mistakes
To be looked upon
With favor and grace
But then I see his face
He doesn't see through my eyes
He sees his favorite
He sees his child
Without shame
And all he wants
Is to embrace
And that she would know
His love for her never fades
He whispers through the shooting stars,
"I'm speaking to your heart
It's for you
To help you see
That you were made for me
And in my eyes I behold
A beauty unfolded
A deep, deep heart
That tears and weeps
And breaks apart

But holds joys dear
And keeps precious memories clear
And I know what you feel
For it is the depth of me
Let me whisper through the stars
But hear it as a scream to the depths of who you are:
You are mine, my child
And you will never leave my arms
My daughter, see as I see
For then you will know you are free
And every face you see
Will be seen through the eyes of me
It is enough
That you belong to me"

Covered

Can you hear the beat of distant drums?
Do they resound inside the reserves of your heart
Rhythm unto rhythm, calling you apart?
The sound is faint to those of Earth
But within Heaven's gates, it erupts like new birth
You can hear if you're still
If you quiet your mind
Inside Heaven's reach your heart is not blind
Can you see a distant light like a star in the night?
Does it speak to your life and call you to rise
Light unto eyes, identifying your drive?
Become who you are
Stare the lie in its face
Remove all your shame and disgrace
For, by one simple embrace
You are covered by blood and stand under grace

Enter In

I enter in, fully clad in battle dress
Though I do not fight with blood and flesh
This war that wages is old and I am new
Born again from a merciful womb
Time stands still as a light in my heart dawns
Awakening both to love and to duty
I bow in love to the King who commissions me
Not to my death but to carry his breath
My waist is girded with Truth,
My chest covered in his righteousness,
My feet shod in peace
Only found within his reach
I am given a shield of fiery faith
Able to defend against every lie from every wraith
My head is guarded by the sturdy steel
Of the salvation that brought me to this field
And last of all, though not least by any measure
I take up the sword of his Word, my dearest treasure
Now, covered head to foot
I'm finally found and ready to begin
As long as I never leave him, I'll win
Wrapped in destiny and favor I'll fight
And his heart will beat in mine
Until the day I die
When I will see him and enter in
With complete delight
Knowing I never gave up the fight

Imagination

You take my imagination to depths beyond fabrication
To places where truth has wings, where simplicity sings
In anticipation of the harmony that accompanies
Your voice
Deeper and deeper still my heart puts down its roots

Into this soil that you till, a cultivation of saturation
Because even in my immaturity, you turn me over
And dig out the jewels in me
And my imagination becomes reality when I see
That you created every compartment of my heart and
When I put words to the page, they create
Life
Movements that pave healing paths in souls that were once
Destined for the grave
Songs that emblaze streams of hope as the pages
Are turned
And one by one as the story moves on
Each recipient finds an education like
New nations springing up inside,
Areas they didn't know were meant to come alive,
Wounds they didn't know could ever heal
And as words go out from these inventions from your mouth
They motivate the wanderer to come home,
Reconcile the divided to come back as one
Because you are the one who weaves our stories
The atonement for our behavior,
You rectify and set right injustice,
Open eyes that have been blind
Imagination is more than fiction
Because in its very diction it can
Bring life where there once was friction and division
God, may these words go forth and reveal your love,
Devotion, and forgiveness

Dreams
When I stare at a blank document,
The cursor doesn't curse and taunt me
I don't see something white and empty
I see a possibility

FLOWERS IN THE DARKNESS | DENICA MCCALL

And the blinking black line winks at me,
Dares me to believe that words yet to be
Can change the present reality
See, I don't believe in impossibility
I believe in dreams
And when we hold onto our dreams
And dream with the One who made them to be,
The One who breathes on our weak attempts
And makes something happen, or helps us connect
When we don't let go when we can't see,
When we let our minds expand with possibilities,
And allow our hearts to swell with what could be,
Something happens
It may just be a seed starting to grow, barely visible, barely known
But over time, you can see green
And you begin to see fruit from all the watering
You start to look and look more closely
As all your dreams become your reality
And the little seed that started in your head
Has become a tree instead
See, I don't believe in limitations
Because a man blew off all the lids a long time ago
Called us to follow him and go where he goes
And where he goes, you never know what you'll get
Healing from pain or a mountain that moves
He's handed you the invitation and you just have to choose
See, I don't believe in boundaries
Because the One who came to set us free broke every one
When death met defeat
And if not even death can hold back a dream,
What's to keep us from following his lead?
When I look at something blank, I no longer see lack
No, what I see is real estate
An investment to be made

An opportunity to bleed onto the page
To create something that hasn't yet been made
When I see the road ahead I don't see the obstacles, but instead
I see a path to blaze
A chance to start something new
Something that makes a difference
See, instead of being indifferent to the things that need to change
Because it's too hard to process the evil taking place
I choose to see a way out of the pain
If I know my Savior dreamed so big he tore the veil so we could
enter in
What's to keep me from dreaming with him?
See, I don't see difficulties
I see potential
For dreams to become reality

Follow Me
Can you hear
Our Creator's call?
He's crying out
"Follow me!"
But only those
Whose eyes can see
Whose ears can hear
Will hear the sound
Of his cry in the air
"Follow me!
You are my bride!
My delight,
Can you sense your destiny?
It's calling you
As it is calling me
Do not fear
Do not feed on hopelessness
I am here
As I have always been
I, your lover

The one you celebrate
Day and night
My faithful ones,
You've never lost sight
Of the reason
You were put on this Earth
And now, follow me
As we march above the fray
For this is the day
My lovers will hear me say,
You are home
Do not delay
The time is ripe
Hear the noise of battle
I have already won this fight!
There may be sorrow
There may be pain
But reward awaits
Those who do not stray
So keep your eyes ahead,
Follow me when all you see is death
Be swallowed in the depths
Of my laughter
Dry your tears,
Put aside your questions
And your many fears
I have not abandoned you all these years
Here I am
On my steed of white
Come to capture
My glorious bride
Follow me!"

Above

Take us above
Lead us beyond
Let us forget this pain,
Leave behind our bonds!
You took it all,
It's done, it's over

Now we can live in your overcoming power

But the hurt is real,
The darkness stings,
These doubts, they steal
From who we are meant to be

"Write, fly! Let it all go!
Let me give you my sweet tears
But take away all your fears
The pain is not yours to hold,
So let my love and joy unfold
Dance, run, smile, and just be
The child you are to me

Hold my heart
Near to yours
Protect it, my child
With innocence, with calm,
With peace in this war,
For nothing can touch you
When there is no fear and no shame
Imprinted on your glorious face"

Journey

Take the journey,
I've made a way
You can't see too far ahead
But I am already there
Knowing every care,
Every hurt, every blow
To your heart along the road
I felt it, too, when I took the journey
Long ago
I know every break
I know every joy
I can't bear it when I see
The times you don't believe
For it pains you
And it was never meant to be

FLOWERS IN THE DARKNESS | DENICA MCCALL

Believe, child
Stand up
Keep walking
Soon you will fly
Because there is victory
In the blood I shed
Walk through the dark night
Look to the day!
Only brightness lies ahead
Rise above the fray!

All you have to do
Is seek my hand
Take it, hold on
And I will never let go
And you will see my face
And you will live by my grace
Until your journey
Is filled with my delight

For all you see
Is my fiery gaze,
The all-consuming fire
The First and the Last
I remain
So fix your eyes
On the Holy One
Who bore your shame,
And this life
Will not leave you lame

Father's Stand

Your hand inside of mine,
I stand here by your side
My heart beats next to your chest
In me will you find rest

My tears are falling down
And cleansing every wound
Let them touch your cheek

And soak you to the core

My love enwraps you
Like a white flowing robe,
Like a river of raging waters
Engulfing every son and daughter

Your hand inside of mine,
I will never let you go
You are always mine,
And I am always who I am

So never be afraid,
Just look into my eyes,
And wonder at the love,
The love that never dies

All the Way

Express your heart to me
Let it run free
Be who I've called you to be
Don't let anything deter you
Let it go
For what can they do to you?
Set them free by living in my truth
When desire comes,
Don't push it down
For you have heard the sound
Of my heart
And when you do,
Nothing can stop you,
For you have beheld a piece
Of who I am
So fall into me
And go all the way
Don't be afraid,
Because there is no shame,
And my heart beats for you to receive
Everything you know you want to believe

The Fullness

Imagine a place with no limits, no end to grace
Imagine a sky full of colors no one has seen,
A green that's way different from the trees,
A blue that's deeper than the sea
Imagine laughter being a color
And tears being a stream
Imagine fire resting on every heart
And dancing that starts when it ends
Imagine a love that never grows faint
And a peace that an artist can paint
Imagine a writer's pen spelling out
The heartbeat of Heaven itself
Imagine a unity so pure
That by our very gathering walls fall down!
This is my song,
It's the song etched on my face,
It's the love that bounds from my heart,
And this is what I want to impart!

Replacement

A moment's embrace
To shield your disgrace
I'm giving you my face
Don't listen
Stop now
Before you shed a tear
I'm here
I've already paid the price
Let me cover you with my wounds
And heal your heart
You are precious to me
And I want you to be free,
So stay with me
Ability comes from my throne
So let me bestow

FLOWERS IN THE DARKNESS | DENICA MCCALL

My favor to flow
Dance in my heart
It's beating for you
The drums of war
Drowning out the enemy's call
Fall into my eyes
I wear no disguise
I will not confuse
Or bring you demise
Trust me
It will set you free
To dance the dance of victory
Confident, holy, set apart
Mine from the very start
That's who you are
And you are never too far

Section IV. Overcoming Struggles and Shortcomings

Most of these poems were created out of moments in my life when I felt discouraged or disappointed, or times I gave into fear or felt weighed down by weakness and failure. Many of them end in words affirming God's goodness and faithfulness to heal, forgive, and love even in the midst of my pain or mistakes. He is always good. I pray you can relate to some of these words and let God lead you in your own process of healing and trusting him again no matter what you may be facing.

<u>Whole and Healed</u>
The darkness seeps in like a thief in the night
Overtaking the light, silent without a fight
How can it win, when I'm hidden in him?
I question this life, this hope, why I live
And confusion creeps in, telling me I'll always sin
I hear the lies but no words, they just shape my life
Overcome by deception, no way out of my plight
Where is the Truth? Does what I'm hearing have proof?
Where to turn, where to look
You say your face is everywhere, but I can't see it

Then you reach down, grab my darkened heart

117

So I know you never left, I just felt we were apart
The light blazes, instantly overtaking the darkness
It stands no chance when my mind and heart believe
When I can see again, and hope remains my friend
Your love always pulls me through, I know I can trust you
With every broken piece, every false identity
For when you speak the Truth, I hear and I declare
That I am different than what I thought, 'cause those were only
lies
You'll never leave my side, I'll follow you to the end
Jesus, you'll always be my Brother and my closest Friend
The One I can rely on, lean on, depend on
And your light, your Truth, will trump the darkness that tries to
steal
The life you've given me through your blood, which can never be
concealed
In you, I am whole and healed

Beautiful

Dry, crusty ground
No life to be found,
She kneels down, undone
Surrendered, broken, her head to the dust
Tears break through
And wet the desolate earth,
A tiny sign of life

Her heart speaks:
I am broken
A daughter, yes, but I see what I am
Without him

My pulse lacks life
Unless he is near
I cannot fear
I cannot hide
I must embrace exposure
And let your life grow inside

A simple breath,

FLOWERS IN THE DARKNESS | DENICA MCCALL

She knows he's near
All around is lifelessness
But he whispers in her ear
This whisper produces hope
And where once a tear had soaked the ground
A stem begins to appear

A sign of life!
She can hardly believe
That Father could grow
Something out of her zero point

Slowly she rises
Aching, but looking towards
Her source of life
He shines down light
And her eyes come alive

She lifts one arm,
Now the other
Her feet shift and begin to move
Now she's spinning
Laughter overtaking her
And the stem becomes a flower

As she dances around,
It grows higher
And shoots colors
She's never known
Into the atmosphere
Until everywhere
There is life and growth

She dances now in freedom
Her smile aglow
Basking in the beauty
That only he could have made
Out of the broken shell that once was her grave

Cover

119

FLOWERS IN THE DARKNESS | DENICA MCCALL

What do you see?
What do you see??
Do you see my heart beating?
I feel it is dead
It is dead without him
So please don't see me

My weakness so plain
It weighs on my soul
But why do I care
If it's for you, I'm told?

I want to be held
I want to be loved
I can only do so much
I've got to give up

Being loved is enough
Knowing him is enough
I want to please him,
But I already do

My heart must believe
My soul must give in
To his relentless faithfulness
In the face of my reckless sin

My heart is so hard
I have a critical eye
I have negative words
My flesh needs to die

But you never fail
You're strong and unmoved
So I am still used

I can't comprehend
Your love so vast
It's hard to believe
That you look past

But I guess to be
A good person at all
I've got to believe
That you are my All

Fill

The pain wrought by life
Inflicting desperate souls
Tires aching hearts
So who can find their home?

No place where we belong
The love we find soon grows old
When will it ever stop?
Surrounded, why do we feel alone?

Pressed in on every side
Fake smiles exchanged, implying hope
Touches linger for moments
We wish we could hold

But we lose our grip before we can
Understand what it's for
The memories fade
And somehow only pain remains

We look for something real
Every day, a search
But by the setting of the sun
We forget why we even started

What can fill our aching hearts?
Who will hold us when we hurt?
Are we doomed to emptiness all our days?
Or is there hope that lingers, a sun with lasting rays?

Why would this question remain
If there's not an answer?
Why do our hearts awaken
If no hope exists?

121

The calling of our Maker
Resounds inside each soul
We won't find rest until
We know he is our home

So let him love you now
Tell him how you feel
When you open up,
Every wound he will heal

He's calling out your name
It is not you who can save
His mercy chooses, in pain
To reach to you

Give your life to him
And your suffering will not be in vain
For he is worth the tears
And he'll remain, through all your years

Where I'm Meant to Be

Without you, I am lost
I won't count the cost
I won't even jump in
In being safe, I think I win
But why do I feel disturbed?
Why am I not at rest
When I hold back,
When I don't let my heart be tested?
I'm born for danger
I was made for risk
Your purpose is my calling
It costs a lot
But I can do nothing less
Save me from myself
Help me flee from safety
For if I don't get out of the boat
I'll be handicapped for life
Imprisoned by mere thoughts

Lies that only have power
If they are believed
The Truth is where I stand
Therefore I can walk hand in hand
With you, Father
Confident, fearless
Stepping out at every chance
Living out my destiny
And held close to your heart
I in you and you in me
This is where I'm meant to be

I'll Stand

To the end
I'll stand
Even when my failure
Threatens me
Beats me up
Leaves me for dead,
I'll stand
I won't give up
When the fight inside overwhelms,
When I can't get over my pride,
I'll remember the one who died
And I'll stand
When anguish tears at my soul,
And I don't know where to go,
Or even what I feel,
I'll look to my Solid Rock
Wave the freedom banner high
And not give up
To the end,
To the end I'll stand
Even when lies become my truth,
I'll deny their power
And look to the Book
That has all the answers
I'll stand
Hand in hand

123

With my God
Whose love will sustain me
Through every up and down
Every joy and pain
'Till the end I'll stand

I Don't Have to Understand

My heart, it beats with one desire
Or how I want it to
Is it truly ripped in two
Or do I just feel what I'm supposed to?
Are we to go about our lives
In either boring days
Or endless pain
And accept it as it comes?
Or is there a way to live and die,
Suffering at a great price
But taking great delight
In the One we love the most?
Should I cease my questioning heart,
My longing mind
And realize
That to live is to die
Even if dying means separation?
Separate, but don't lose my heart
Allow the pain
Because it's worth it?
I won't shut down
I'll feel what he wants me to feel
After all
I love him the most
But just don't let me boast
In myself
And don't let me stray
And get in the way
Firm trust
In the midst of storms
My heart no longer dead
Nor fearing the norm

Or the empty
Because life with you,
Life for you
Has no comparison
To anything else
I don't understand
This life
But you gave it to me
So I'll trust
When I don't know where to go
No belonging,
No clear future
You are my home
And I'll follow
The cadence
Of your sweet voice

Imperfection

Glaring imperfection,
Frustrated desire
Am I a reflection
Of all you inspire?
You've breathed the breath of life
Into my molded lungs
You still the restless fight
Wash my darkened heart; that's why you hung
Now you're holding me together
With your arms so strong
You carry me through stormy weather
And spin me with your song
You want to be so close,
I want the same thing, too
I want a deeper dose
Of what my King's been through
I know what you did for me
But I want to know your heart
God, please let me see
In whole instead of part
Let me be your work of art,

125

A shining reflection of what you impart
To be the dream of God
Draw me in; here's my heart

Tired

My soul can't find a resting place
'Till it is home in your embrace
Your heart fulfills my restless desire
Your touch is my life; it's how I'm wired

Father, I'm tired
I'm tired of going on my own
Tired of my anger, my throne
Abba, I can't go this alone
I'm falling every second I can't see home
My heart is calloused, mind shut down
When silence is rejection and my thoughts, they bow

God, I don't want to judge
I don't want to be proud
The enemy is after my identity
And if I let him steal my thoughts, he'll drag me down

I'm called to love no matter what
Not live within this selfish rut
God, right now I ask you, please
To wash my heart and fill me with your peace
Dust away the broken pieces
And give me a heart that stands
For everything that you believe in
Make me a child again
So I can fearlessly command
Demons to flee far from these lands

Father, you are my home
That will never change
My soul will wander all night and day
Until it finds your arms and stays
I can't do this on my own
Catch me now, because I am letting go

126

Take me where you want me to go
The places where I have to fly to get there
And your breath is my only air

I Need Grace

I admit that I don't care
But the desire is still there
People need you, God, and I
Only think of my own life
A sinner, stripped and bare
But you chose me your love to share
First you poured it in
'Till I was full to the brim
But now I'm hungry again
Because I haven't shared so I can let more in
You have a lot of love for me to give
That is what I know
I won't put on a show,
I'll live
To give it all away
And for this I need your grace

Broken Life

Do you despise
My broken life?
Because all I see sometimes
Are these scattered pieces
And the lies
Is this what defines
My existence?
These selfish thoughts,
This pride that robs
Me of what my heart longs for,
To be loved and adored?
But I go about it my way
Which is always the worst
Instead of making you first
The pieces are everywhere
Here, there,
In the past and near to my heart

Fragmented memories
Building the story of my life here
But I'm only torn apart
Because I keep drifting away
Pulled down and losing my way
Forgetting this love you've put in my heart
This passion in my veins
Is darkened
And I live my life in vain
I need to see your eyes
Every day, every night
Remind me who I am
And let your love command
My soul to be still
And rest in your steady plan
And see the weaving from your hand
For you have made
Something beautiful out of my days
Let it be forever for your praise

When I Don't Know What to Do

I know I do it wrong
But what can I do?
When I look at me,
I'm not like you
I know it shouldn't be
I know that I am free
But when will I find peace?
I know I need to change
I know that they do, too
But focusing on them
Is not what will get me through
I know the Truth
I know deep down what I desire
But will I let this fire
Stir within and cause a move?
What is my destination?
And what is in the way?
Is it people and their problems
Or is it the way I let them stay?

I know your eyes are steady
I know your love is true
I know what's real, I just forget
To keep my eyes on you
Knowing is one thing
But do I believe?
Do I believe enough in change
That I'll take a step to prove my faith?
It all comes back to you
And when I don't know what to do,
I can look into your eyes
And you'll reveal that it's a lie
I know
Because I believe
I believe in a love so deep
That can keep me in the arms of my King
Through everything
I'm not who I'm meant to be
But I know you can make me
Because I believe
In an undying love that has set me free

Craving

In the depths of my soul, there's a place they can't fill
As much as I hunger, yet I hunger still
In the pit of my heart, there's a vein that has started
To pump through blood that can't be satiated
Until it covers and consumes
Until it flows through
Every bone in my body, until it meets you

This craving inside me, I hide it so well
Until all my yearnings starve and I fall
I fall at your feet, drown in your eyes
Just so I can find the life, the life
Of your Word, the passion that lets my oldness die
And your Holy Ghost inside to awaken

FLOWERS IN THE DARKNESS | DENICA MCCALL

Let it through, let it through, I cry day and night
For hunger that is broken is useless
Let it come, let it come, I scream through my pride
For self in its thirst is empty and uptight

I want what is right
Can't you see that even what I hold so tight,
What I'm afraid to let go, I want you to take
Because for your sake I want to see what's at stake

My appetite for you is the only one that never dies
It fights through the nights
When every cell is awake
And won't give me rest until I'm near you and take
Your heart into mine, your life in my lungs
Your blood infusing my arteries
To show me true sacrifice
And what my days mean
To give you praise, to worship in grace
To prostrate my heart
To see your face

Undo my disgrace at not recognizing true faith
Repair me again in your love,
Take me again up above
I come to your table a starving beggar
So hungry, I'll fall without shame at your feet
And wash them with the stains of my past
That you look at then give me your hand
So we can step into your future, your plan

There's a place in my soul they can't satisfy
Only when I receive what I know in your eyes

Set Free

When you say to chase them away,
What does that mean?
Because all the demons tell me they're here to stay
That they'll have their way
I don't see a path to chase them down
The way is blocked all around
We're locked together in this arena of soul and spirit
And I will fight because I must,
For her soul the Father must inherit
But how,
When the voices scream so loud
I can't even hear you?
When their taunting seems so proud
They ignore you?
But see, the difference between me and them
Is that I choose to hear you,
I understand
That your love makes a way
Through their violent threats of death
And none of them can get away
Once I speak your name
With confidence and
The authority you've given me
So the demons have to flee
You send your angels as reinforcement
And she is set free

Source

How much time can I waste
Thinking I have no words to say?
I'm on the edge of disgrace
Tears threatening to streak down my face

131

I've lost sight of your grace
In this moment
When all inside me wants to live with meaning,
I sit around idly and can't feel you
I know you haven't left
Because if you had, I'd have tasted death
But why do I sit here, lonely
When you've given me your voice?
And I always have a choice
I need your love, what can I say?
I'm an orphan here, just waiting for that day
When I'll know I'm wanted
I don't mean to say I'm ungrateful
Or that it's not true
By my heart doesn't always feel as it should
Until I pursue yours
So teach me, Father
As I sit here, without words
Scraping and scrounging, trying to discern
What it's all about
I'm lost just like all the rest
I have nothing your mercy hasn't sent
So keep me humble and keep me open
But don't let me forget that I don't have to be broken
Forever
Hold me now, hold me close
I want to hear your breath, the bob of your throat
I need to know your warmth, your soft, gentle voice
That steals all the lies, that hushes the chaos
In my mind
You're stirring in my life
I'm coming away with you
For what else can I do
In the midst of this pain,

In the midst of all we're going through?
You're the anchor to my soul
The rose that teaches me to unfold
The warrior that opposes all my foes
And brings me near to your kingly throne
The words are there, barely scratching the fringes of your
presence
But do my eyes see?
Open,
Open up
Climb deep inside and show me
Who you are
How life speaks and points to you
As the source
Father, hear my prayer
Your daughter's waiting here
Not knowing what to ask
But not satisfied without your touch

The Life You Give

My heart as cold as ice
A slippery slope of blindness
Unwilling to yield until it breaks
Under the crushing weight of guilt
Oh, my unreliable witness
To the events in my life
My eyes see something not there
But are veiled to the truth of your life
My filter only yields
What I expect or surmise from the past
But it's not a true grid
Of your faithful perspective
Melt my heart to see
That it's not guilt you bestow upon me

FLOWERS IN THE DARKNESS | DENICA MCCALL

When I question all I've thought is right,
Bring me back to your side
And tell me it's alright
I can be broken and still speak
I can be shattered and still move
Un-relying on my shame
But composing for your name
My heart tells lies I can't deny
But confusion only reigns
When I let it steal your fame
So help me to give in
To your words, not my sin
Then and only then
Can I be free to live the life you give

What It's About

As I come to the temple, I find that my idol is not only blind
But dead
And what I had conjured up in my head only served to make a
bed
For fear
So when I tried to draw near, my heart just switched gears
And distraction became a shroud over your name
And even your face was distant
And even in my insistence I couldn't feel your kisses
Because my heart had grown cold
Unfeeling, ashes the only reminder of a fire that once was
burning
When I tried to rekindle, I only could see the face of my idol
Until my faith dwindled and what once was crazy love
Turned into the dull mundane,
A gathering spent lauding your name
But a heart longing for joy instead of this pain
And then you came to me

Showed me what you intended,
The creativity you structured to make my heart come alive
And beauty unfurl, bringing hope to the world
Worshipping your majesty is the only thing I'm made to do
And when I turn from the fear and the doubt and the idols that
Make me forget what life's about,
I can see you again and love is all my heart will shout

I Am Undone

Oceans of love wait outside my door
But the inside is locked with my chest to the floor
My restless heart beats against this cage
As the waves beat and rage
Against the door that may as well be
An open book for you to read

Yet you wait for me to grab the key
And unlock the inside of my cell
Because, you say, I'm already free
But it's my choice what I will believe,
If I'm destined for bliss or deserving of Hell

The rush of the waters reaches my ears
The sounds lingering and bouncing off four walls
Beckoning me with notes of love igniting tears
A longing I've had but not acknowledged through many tainted
years

All my fears rush to my head
I reach out my hand, desperate for release
Stretch my mouth wide but I can't even scream
My heart just swells with the sensation until all I see is red

Then in my demise you show me your eyes

And your scars come into my view
In your presence begins the termination of all these lies
You touch and you heal and start making me new

I stand up, grab hold of the key that always sat right in front of
me,
Run to the door and unlock the barrier
That used to separate my heart from this torrent of love
The waters rush over me and I finally feel free
I'm swept away in my exchange and I know you're my carrier
I want to drown in the waves until I am undone

Enough

Your nearness defeats my feelings
My will can be so unyielding and yet, when I surrender you
conceal me
When I congeal my heart your hand moves me and heals every
part
That wants to say life is not good enough, that I'm tired of all
this stuff
That pours wantonly into my life, creating heartache and strife
But your whisper always brings me back
So I can face every attack
With confidence through my tears, knowing you're faithful all of
my years
Your promise is true even when I don't believe you
And that's the beauty of your point of view
My eyes are blind, this world limits my sight
But you are there before me, paving paths in the night
I feel your hand intertwine with mine until my soul unwinds
And peace remains, because in the shelter of your name
Tempests may brew and my dreams may be wasted
But your embrace tells me I've only just tasted
A drop of what you have waiting for me just outside that gate

And all I have to do is trust that my life's not up to fate
But remains secure even while I wait
Even as war and hell break loose around my vulnerable cell
You break in and tell me all will be well
Your breath, your whisper, your touch of love
Surrounds my being and envelops my thoughts
And you, here and now, are all I'll ever want
You're enough

Joy

Hope rushes in like a thief in my night
Stealing what binds and the grief and the strife
Like a welcome intruder hacking into my computer
To spread the virus of joy to every part of my life

Grace comes to me like a pleasant surprise
Reminds me who I am and why I'm alive
Washes and renovates and recreates all my insides
So that I'm stirred and broken all over again
When I see that you win over all of my sin

My world has this tendency to play on my fragility
To take all that's weak and unsure and dress it up
Then put me in front of a mirror to see all that's corrupt
To take what's broken and painful around and inside
And blow it up in my face to make my innocence die

But you gave me this faith to have new eyes to see
To see that what's around me is not definitive reality
But to see that in the midst of the hardships and valleys
Your love surrounds and fills and sets our hearts free

Hope is my anchor to keep me on top of the waves
Joy I hold onto because even in the face

137

Of pain and tears and years and years of waiting
You hold onto me and are writing this story of beauty
And I will be with you for eternity

When I know and I think of forever with you,
There's nothing in the world that can tear me from this view
And all I want to do is go deeper in your heart
So that I can impart the truth of who you are
To a people desperate for hope, void of joy
See, what they lack is right before them, they just need to know
And be aware of our enemy's ploy
Your love, the hope of our world, the freedom for every heart
This is my joy that fuels my life and my art
This joy that is not only attainable but accessible
To walk in, to breathe in, to live out your parable

I Came to the Shore

I came to the shore, and I said I can't handle this anymore
I have to know what this is all about, why the people shout
About your wild heart, why they see flying colors in the air
And turn into children when your breath lingers there
I have to know why certain things are forbidden and dark
And what is in me that is drawn to them
I have to know of this evil in my heart that takes my curiosity
And drives me to insanity
So I came to the shore
To see what all these people come here for
Every night, just to gather in one place; is it the beauty they adore
Or is there more?
I gazed out across the ocean—blue-green waves topped with
sparkling diamonds
Lapping lazily at the sand, covering feet, and
For those on their knees, hungry hands
I looked as many lay stricken, as smiles spread from ear to ear

And I wondered what they felt, what they heard, what could steal
away their fear
Because all my life I lived with fear, always running, never home
Was it the darkness inside I tried to escape?
Or some outside force that I couldn't name?
I took a step closer to the edge of the water, and it seemed to
vibrate with eager tremors
What power was this, what spell was it under?
Then the pull was too strong, and I dived right under
The water engulfed me on every side
I thought I made a mistake, and so I cried out, fear racking my
frame
I called out, I wanted to be unmade
Pain split through every pore in my body
I thought I would die—this power, it had me
Then everything calmed as I heard the one word—
My name, spoken softly, in a voice I'd never heard
But somehow, though foreign, in that whisper I sensed
That the person who owned this voice had been with me since
my birth
It didn't make sense, and for the first time
It didn't have to when that voice said, "You're mine
I love you, I want you, I want you to be
With me forever, drowning in this love that you see"
My whole frame was rocked, I'd been gut-punched with love
And pleasure rolled through me 'till I was undone
I felt like a child, out of control
But in the release I knew I was whole
Enclosed by this water that held me with love
I was a new person, recreated with love

Section V. Who God Is

There are only two poems in this section, and I believe they are a proper conclusion. I wrote the first one on Good Friday as an exploration of what God really did for us, and how his love shouts to us through the Cross. God's heart is love. It's that simple. The second one is essentially my testimony, which points to nothing else but God's great love proven true in the midst of my own broken life.

The Heart of God
God kissed
A merciless world

God suffered
As a man
Humiliated, broken
Separated, abandoned
To let himself feel
The pain of rejection
But the unmatchable joy
Of a heart given

The heart of God
Breaks
But his love knows
It's worth the cost

We spit in his face
We shame him every day

140

What do we know of love?
When will we see his face?

The passion of God
Will not relent
Until all his would-be enemies
Have been forgiven
Until all his followers
Turn from their hypocritical ways

The blood of God
Was spilled
And freely spent
To show a lost world
What it means to live

It hurts more to forgive
Than to die
And that's what he does
Every day
His pain has not gone away
Yes, victory is his
But people still choose

We shun him,
We forget him,
We reject and abuse him,
Yet he hunts us down
He heals our wounds
He knows our pain,
Gathers our tears
And his love continues to set us free

The heart of God
Is displayed
Every day
Can you begin to see
The longing in his heart
For you, his dear child?

Your love
Is worth more to him
Than anything

It's the heart of God
Who kissed the very ones
Who denied him,
Defiled him
And killed him
But his love remains the same

When I Woke

When I woke from the dream of my pale, empty life
And came face to face with all my disgrace
I cried in the night, mourning my plight
To be seen and be known when I couldn't see light
I had known the right answers, my mind proved them true
But the one thing missing was you

When I woke from the lies that were shocking my hopes
Into dead, futile dreams of a child who couldn't cope,
When I saw that my world was much bigger than me,
I gave you the keys

Your nearness blasted through the walls I never knew
Enveloped my blindness, told me I was new
Your whispers of love broke every chain
And I could see that my life would never be in vain

See, you bled from your veins
A sacrifice too deep for words
And if I were to discard or discredit its worth
You would have died, and I, a prisoner would remain,
A slave to the pain of this Earth

But your love conquers all
It ruptured every wall
Until all I could do was fall
When you looked into my eyes

FLOWERS IN THE DARKNESS | DENICA MCCALL

And stayed until I denied every lie

In my flight in the night
When I wanted to give up this fight
You came and you held me tight,
When I woke from the dream, your Truth was what lingered
Like edges of hope lining my heart with your Word

FLOWERS IN THE DARKNESS | DENICA MCCALL

Keep In Touch

If you're interested in joining Denica on her writing journey (including staying up-to-date on the latest news about upcoming novels), here are some ways to connect:

Website: denicamccall.com
Facebook: Denica McCall, Writer
Twitter: @MDenica

www.ingramcontent.com/pod-product-compliance
Lightning Source LLC
Chambersburg PA
CBHW061827040426
42447CB00012B/2854